N Watt

Return items to **any** Swindon library by closing
time on or before the date stamped. Only books
and Audio Books can be renewed - phone your
library or visit our website.
www.swindon.gov.uk/libraries

North Swindon
Library 9/11
Tel: 01793 707120

Copying recordings is illegal. All recorded items
are hired entirely at hirer's own risk

D1440078

www.susanjeffers.com

DARE TO CONNECT

HOW TO CREATE CONFIDENCE, TRUST AND LOVING RELATIONSHIPS

SUSAN JEFFERS

piatkus

PIATKUS

First published in Great Britain in 1992 by Piatkus Books
First mass market paperback edition published in 1995 by Piatkus Books
This paperback edition published in 2011 by Piatkus

A CIP catalogue record for this book
is available from the British Library

ISBN 978-0-7499-4122-2

Printed and bound in the UK by
CPI Mackays, Chatham ME5 8TD

Papers used by Piatkus are from well-managed forests
and other responsible sources.

MIX
Paper from
responsible sources
FSC   FSC® C104740
www.fsc.org

Piatkus
An imprint of
Little, Brown Book Group
100 Victoria Embankment
London EC4Y 0DY

An Hachette UK Company
www.hachette.co.uk

www.piatkus.co.uk

Acknowledgments

As I write these acknowledgments, I am reminded of the tremendous amount of support, caring and love that exists in my life. I am truly grateful.

Dominick Abel, my agent, who gently reminds me when I need to hear it that 'it's all happening perfectly!' His friendship is so welcome in my life. Thank you, Dominick.

Mandi Robbins, my assistant and friend, who made my life flow so that I could write this book with peace of mind. Her loyalty and gentleness are welcome gifts to this world. Thank you, Mandi.

The men and women who generously shared their feelings with me about love, friendship and the workplace. They have truly made a difference in your life and mine by sharing who they are. Thank you, beautiful people.

The men and women who let me know that my work has touched their lives. Their feedback so greatly touches and inspires me. Thank you, beautiful people.

My wonderful friends, who support the very best that I can be. With such great friends, life is a banquet. Thank you, dear friends.

My children, stepchildren and their spouses: Gerry . . . Leslie and Michael . . . Guy and Ashley . . . Alice and Anthony.
All of them have lovingly expanded my world and I respect and admire who they are. Thank you, my wonderful family.

Joyce Shelmerdine, my mother-in-law, who has welcomed me into her heart. I will always be grateful. Thank you, Joyce.

Marcia my sister, with whom I share a bond of love and light that grows deeper every day . . . and her wonderful husband, **Bruce**, who is a gift to my life . . . and to this world. Thank you, Marcia and Bruce.

Joyce and Dick Shelmerdine, my parents-in-law, who welcomed me into their hearts. I will always be grateful. Thank you, Joyce and Dick.

Mark Shelmerdine, my incredible husband. His contribution to my life is felt so deeply within my being. Our love grows and grows. Thank you, my dearest Mark.

and

Jeanne and Leon Gildenberg, my mother and father, who, while no longer here in body, are always with me in spirit. Thank you, Mom and Dad. I miss you.

Contents

THE SOUL OF CONNECTION

To my children
Gerry Gershman and Leslie Wandmacher
On their journey towards wholeness, they have
taught me so much about loyalty, love and life.
My respect, admiration and love are enormous.

And, as always . . .

To the 'miracle' of my husband
Mark Shelmerdine
His support, generosity, wisdom and love never
cease to astound me. I am truly blessed.

Preface for My Readers in Other Countries

I am so pleased to share with you the many ideas I have about how each one of us can ease any loneliness and alienation that exists within our lives . . . with our partners, friends, co-workers and people in general.

While my writing derives primarily from my experiences in the United States, I am very aware of our similarities. I have lived in England for three years and have travelled extensively. In my personal experiences and extensive research, I have learned that too many of us have been well educated in matters of competition, but very badly educated in matters of the heart and soul. The former creates separation; the latter, connection.

We all have the power to create a feeling of warmth and belonging anywhere we go. In order to do so, it is necessary to take a good look at our training and change what doesn't work for us. Within this book, I've included many concepts and ideas to help you on your journey to connection. They will work for you as they have worked for me.

I know that you will say 'yes' to most of my ideas, but since aspects of our culture differ, you may not agree with everything. As always, take what works for you and leave the rest behind. There may also be some phrases or words with which you are not familiar. Not to worry! You won't have any trouble deriving the meaning intended. Having said that, I think you will be amused, surprised, and, most importantly, moved by what I have to say.

I want you to know that while I may never meet you personally, I feel privileged to be a part of your life. As we mutually share more and more of our ideas, our understanding and caring for one another will help close the distances that exist throughout this world. This is my hope, this is my dream.

From my heart to yours,
Susan Jeffers

Introduction

Many times throughout our lives, we experience painful feelings of loneliness and isolation. It would seem that the natural thing to do at such times is simply to reach out and connect with those around us. But as we all know from personal experience, feelings of self-doubt too often make the act of reaching out very difficult, if not impossible. As a result, we remain isolated from the very thing that can ease our pain . . . **the warmth of the human heart.**

Dare to Connect has been written to give you insights and tools to ease any feelings of loneliness and alienation you may have. It provides answers to questions about connection generally, and, more specifically, in the areas of romance, friendship and the workplace. I have been trained in the field of psychology and I have interacted with thousands of people through the internet and in my role as author, workshop leader, public speaker and talk show expert. As a result, I am fairly certain that many of your questions will be similar to the ones I am frequently asked by others. For example:

- Why do I feel so nervous when walking into a room full of strangers?
- How can I pick up the phone and make that sales call without feeling so anxious?
- Why is it hardest to approach the person I'm most interested in meeting?
- Why do I feel so lonely, even though I'm always surrounded by people?
- How can I overcome my fear of rejection?
- How can I make friends?
- How do I read someone else's signals?
- What do I do if someone misreads my signals?
- What do men really want from women (and vice versa)?
- What are the new rules about approaching someone for a date?
- Why can't I ask for help at work where I so often need it?
- Why do I feel so alienated from my husband?

The people who ask these questions represent a huge cross-section of the population – men and women, single and married, young and old, rich and poor, atheists and 'believers' – yet their problems with connection abound. Some want to be married but are locked into devastating insecurity when it comes to approaching a possible partner; some tremble as they walk into a business meeting or approach a potential customer or face an important interview; some ache for friends with whom to share their sadness and joy, yet totally wall themselves in when the opportunity for sharing arises; some are married, but still feel painfully alone.

Feelings of self-doubt and alienation are certainly not foreign to me. There was a time when my lack of confidence created isolation in all areas of my life. The simple act of walking into a crowded room produced butterflies in my stomach, sweaty palms and a pounding heart. I often dealt with my lack of confidence in inappropriate ways, including self-deception. For example, my first job required me to attend many business functions on my own. My habit was to walk into a room, take a look around at all the people who seemed to be happily engaged in conversation, decide everyone was boring . . . and leave as quickly as possible. One day, the obvious question popped into my mind: 'How do I know they're boring when I haven't even talked to them?'

It was then that I came face to face with the underlying truth behind my thoughts and actions. 'What if I introduce myself to someone . . . and they aren't interested in knowing me?' Obviously it was **me** whom I considered boring . . . not them! Thankfully, I can now walk confidently into a crowded room filled with unfamiliar faces. Over the years, I have made many discoveries that allow me to reach out comfortably to others, no matter what the situation. I wrote *Dare to Connect* so that I could share these discoveries.

You may be someone who is comfortable in one arena, but a quivering mass in another. For example, you may find it easy to connect in business and friendship, but not when it comes to romance. Or you may be at ease in social situations, but unable to break the competitive barrier at work so that you and your colleagues could support each others' professional growth. Regardless of your situation, valuable tools in this book will help erase your self-doubt as you move forward to connect with others.

You may wonder how similar concepts and techniques can apply in such diverse situations. Strangely, they do. It won't take you long to discover that tools that bolster our confidence in one area of our lives can't help but improve all other areas as well. For example Tim, a lawyer who attended one of my workshops on relationships, found that the tools he learned for approaching someone of the opposite sex also made facing the judge and jury much easier.

The book is divided into four main sections. **The Heart of Connection** explains why we so often feel like a 'nobody', and then points us in the direction of feeling good about ourselves once again. **The Journey Inward to Connection** explores why we harbour feelings of inadequacy and loneliness and how to eliminate them – thus allowing healthy connection to occur. **The Journey Outward to Connection** presents the basic techniques of connection and those specific to the areas of romance, friendship and business. (Even if you don't feel you have a problem in one or more of these areas, read all the sections. The concepts and tools in one section reinforce those in the others.) Finally, **The Soul of Connection** shows you how to participate in the world in a way that could keep you from ever feeling alienated again.

Many exercises are provided throughout the book. They are meant to be incorporated into your daily life so that self-destructive thoughts are replaced by a healthy way of seeing yourself and the world around you. If you put these exercises into practice, in time, connecting with other human beings will feel like an act of love rather than a scary and potentially humiliating experience!

I suggest that you read through the book once. Then go through it again and again until you 'own' it. Underline, circle, write in the margins; most importantly, make the exercises come to life. People who report the greatest success use my teaching as a starting point and then actually incorporate the tools and concepts into their daily lives. As they have taken on the responsibility of practising how to feel more powerful and loving in their day-to-day interactions, their lives have changed dramatically. Some have left unhealthy relationships or found healthy ones; some have become more successful in their careers; some have found wonderful new friends; some are simply getting more enjoyment out of life now that their insecurity has been replaced by a greater sense of confidence and peace of mind.

As you begin using the tools throughout the book, remember to be patient with yourself. Learn at a comfortable pace, not expecting overnight miracles. You have probably already made the unfortunate discovery that changing negative thinking and behaviour patterns doesn't happen overnight. Change requires constant practice and repetition. Don't dwell on setbacks when they occur (and they will); rather, focus on every little sign of progress. When you hit a snag or a setback in your ability to connect with others, simply pick up the book again and find the section that addresses the difficulty. Positive feelings will reappear, and you can face the world once again.

If you find the voice of impatience creeping in, just keep repeating:

One step at a time is enough for me.

You'll find yourself changing significantly in ways that will allow you to be with others in a more confident and loving way. Above all, **don't give up!** The quality of your life is at stake. You are too important to deprive yourself and others of the power and love you hold within. Sharing ourselves with others gives life meaning and purpose . . . and a feeling of fulfilment and inner peace.

Dare to Connect is not your usual how-to book – it introduces an element that is absent in many well-intentioned books of this nature. I'll let you discover it as you progress. I believe you will be deeply moved and challenged by the book. One of my students told me at the conclusion of a workshop, 'It wasn't what I expected, but it was much more than I could have hoped for.' I hope *Dare to Connect* touches you in the same way.

The Heart of Connection

1

There Are No Strangers

When I was in my twenties, I was friendly with a night club singer who always closed his act with the words: 'The most important thing that I've learned in my travels around the world is that **there are no strangers, only friends I've never met**.' His fans obviously loved it because they always responded to his words with applause, smiles and tears. Being young and sceptical I thought it was pure corn and manipulation, but I couldn't deny that he had touched a chord.

When I was in my thirties, I attended an all-day workshop with seven thousand other people in New York City's Felt Forum. The workshop leader came out on to the stage to face this awesome crowd and, after his opening thank yous, stated, 'I don't know your names, but I know who you are.' I recognized it as another version of my night club singer's message, but, being a bit older and mellower now, I was able to catch the germ of truth in the words. Yes, in many ways we are all the same; we all experience feelings of fear, pain, joy, anger, jealousy, judgment, happiness, sadness, generosity, greed and every other human emotion.

When I was in my forties, I began seeking answers to certain questions that kept coming up in my mind:

> If, in fact, there are no strangers, why do we often feel so separate from everyone around us? Why do we often feel so alone? Why do we often feel like outsiders looking in? If we are alike in so many ways, why do we often feel so inferior?

I ultimately discovered that part of the answer to these questions lies in the way we have been trained to see ourselves relative to other human beings. One of my favourite models of this training process comes from the author and teacher Ram Dass.[1] He suggests that when we are born, we immediately go into **'Somebody Training'**; that is, we are taught by our parents and our society that what we are 'supposed to' be in this world is a Somebody! They define a Somebody as a person who has achieved some measure of *external* success. As a result, our 'Somebody-ness', or self-worth, is dependent on such factors as money, status, power, personality, looks and intellectual excellence.

You might ask, 'What's wrong with that? Isn't our quest to be a Somebody and achieve some measure of external success in the world the source of much of our motivation and drive?' The answer to that is, of course, yes! But when we allow these trappings to become a measure of our self-worth, we set ourselves up for an incredible amount of pain, and instead of feeling like a Somebody, we end up feeling like a Nobody!

There are several reasons for this:

a) Somebody Training emphasizes individual differences and puts us in competition with everyone around us. Hence, we are always on a treadmill trying to keep up with or surpass everyone else . . . or we just give up when the competition seems too great.

b) When we strive to fill ourselves up with approval from people 'out there', we twist the essence of who we really are and create a false picture which we hope will bring us the acceptance we crave. And when we lose sight of who we truly are, we feel empty inside.

c) When we focus only on externals, such as looks, money, success or sex appeal (ours or theirs), we lose sight of our common humanity. We lose sight of the feelings that lie within, of those unseeable qualities that create a feeling of bonding. And we feel alienated.

Our external identity cards have been important from a very early age. Think back to when you were young. How often did you feel like a Somebody and how often like a Nobody? How often did you feel too fat, or too thin, or too dumb, or too tall, or too short, or too loud, or too quiet, or too pushy, or too shy, or too selfish, or too much of a pushover . . . or too whatever? In order to be a Somebody, there was always something to 'fix'.

Even if there was someone in your life who was extraordinarily supportive, I bet you felt like a Nobody a great deal of the time. I did. I remember feeling like a Nobody when I came home from school with my work marked B because my parents believed that Somebodies always got As. I remember feeling like a Nobody when the boy I had a crush on didn't invite me to the school dance. I remember feeling like a Nobody when schoolmates sang 'I don't want her, you can have her. She's too fat for me.'

I was taught by my parents and society that to be a Somebody, one had to be smart (without letting the boys know just how smart), pretty, popular, and the lead in the school play. Of course there were variations, but all of the other girls in my class were programmed in a similar way. Naturally, the boys had their own special brand of Somebody Training; they were supposed to be athletic, tall and handsome.

It didn't stop there. We were also programmed about how to be a Somebody when we grew up. The girls were expected to find a successful husband (which meant a rich and handsome professional man), have a couple of children and be beautiful and adorable all of the time. The boys were expected to marry an attractive woman, get ahead in the workplace and be the protector of the household.

It is true that times have changed since the fifties in terms of social roles and expectations, but nothing much has changed in terms of our Somebody Training. We are still measured by our external achievements. No matter how involved and supportive our parents may have been, no matter how much they built us up and tried to make us feel great about ourselves, it is virtually impossible for us to escape the framework of success set down by our society.

To see how this may have worked within your family unit, you might want to sit down quietly and answer the following questions:

- Who did my parents consider to be a Somebody and what made them so in their eyes?
- Who do I, today, consider to be a Somebody and why?
- What do I think I have to 'fix' within myself or achieve to make me a Somebody?

I suspect that your answers will focus primarily on external rather than internal qualities that have to do with loving, caring and sharing – that is, connection. You will begin to see how much of our early conditioning needs to be reversed in order to topple our walls of isolation.

Incidentally, even those who fit all the external requirements of success seldom feel like a Somebody. Look at the self-destructive lives of Marilyn Monroe, Elvis Presley and John Belushi. In the eyes of the world they were Somebodies, but in the depths of their being they obviously felt as if they were Nobodies. Author and counsellor John Bradshaw sums it up when he says that, because of our conditioning, we all live with a feeling of **toxic shame** (whether we are successful or not), experienced as the pervasive sense of being flawed and defective as human beings.[2] This is hardly a good place from which to form connections in any area of our lives!

Equally devastating to our ability to connect is the way Somebody Training fosters an atmosphere of judgment. He or she isn't rich enough, attractive enough, outgoing enough, generous enough, ambitious enough, kind enough and so on . . . and we put them out of our hearts. We put them down in order to puff ourselves up, not realizing that in the long run hurting others in this way makes us feel even more of a Nobody than we felt before.

While it is important to look at our upbringing to determine what hurtful teachings need to be corrected, it is important that we don't blame our parents. 'Why not?' you say. 'Look what they did to us!' In the first place, blaming is a powerless act. It creates a feeling of helplessness instead of trust in our own ability to create a healthy sense of self. Secondly, our parents probably did the best they could, given their own upbringing. Were they not also a product of Somebody Training? Isn't their behaviour, no matter how distressing and inappropriate, the result of their own struggle against feelings of worthlessness as they made their way in the world?

Sadly, I realize that in the name of love I did many of the same kind of hurtful things to my children as my parents did to me. And I observe other caring parents also trying very hard to do what's 'best' for their children. Unfortunately, in a Somebody-Trained world, that usually means correcting, moulding, shaping, changing and so on, until what's left of the child is a master actor who may look like a Somebody but feels like a Nobody. And Mummy and Daddy sit there applauding their handiwork (or wondering where they went wrong), not realizing they've lost their real child and created a fake.

Schools seldom help. I remember seeing a bulletin board in the hall of a primary school on which all the pupils were ranked according to their marks. Imagine the effect on the children's self-esteem. If the child who was number one dropped to second place, he or she couldn't help but feel like a loser – after all, he or she was no longer 'the best'. But my heart went out most of all to the children at the bottom of the list. I wonder how many of them cried themselves to sleep every night at the prospect of facing that telling list the next morning.

It is amazing how psychologically numb our entire social structure is to the feelings of children. Take a look at children with their teachers or parents in the local playground – it's a real eye-opener! The number of negative messages that the adults give to the children is staggering! And even as adults, everywhere we turn we are reminded of our imperfections. For example, advertisers in magazines and the media sell us illusions which we will never be able to achieve in life. The puzzling fact is that we put up with it.

What this all means is that if we are conditioned to focus only on the external packaging, whether it's someone else's or our own, separation and loneliness will inevitably prevail and we end up with a society of what's been called 'empty suits'. And on it will go forever . . . **unless we change the training**. The question is, how do we go about that?

Part of the answer lies in acknowledging that, while there is nothing inherently wrong with wanting to improve the externals of our life *per se*, our sense of connection with ourselves and the people around us does not come from externals. Rather it comes from learning how to find that place within us all where **we always feel like a Somebody** and where **we perceive everybody else as a Somebody**, thus completing the circle of connection. There is no competition, only compassion. There is no fear, only love. There is no hate, only caring. (Sounds like Heaven, doesn't it?)

Those of you who are familiar with my previous books know that I am talking about the place called the Higher Self. From this transcendent place it is possible to break down the walls of separation and

bring us into harmony with ourselves and each other.
There is no question in my mind that

> It is in the Higher Self that we find the
> Heart of Connection.

If you are uncomfortable with the mention of the
Higher Self, thinking it might have something to do
with religion or God, take note that I am referring
only to the inner spiritual part of our being, the best
of who we are – the part of us that is loving, compassionate, caring, giving, abundant, creative, intuitive and
knows there is nothing to fear. So whether you believe
in God or not, the model will work for you.

The Higher Self, in the way I am using the term, is
familiar to *all* of us even though we may not have
labelled it as such. We experience the Higher Self
during those times when we realize that 'we are all in
it together'. For example, when we attend an event
that is raising money to feed the hungry, we feel part
of the collective human heart. Or when we pull
together at a time of crisis, we rise above the level of
our individual differences and we stop competing. For
those brief moments in time, the externals of our life,
which usually seem so important, appear petty and
unimportant as we touch a more noble place within.

Given that the Higher Self describes a place that
exists within all of us, and given that the Higher Self
is the place where we feel connected to the whole
human race (including the attractive person across
the room with whom we would love to have dinner!),
the important question is this. How do we get there
from here in our everybody lives?

The answer is that we need to enter into a new kind

of training. I suggest we call it **Everybody Training**. The exercises in this new kind of training are designed to give us the strength to make the transition from Somebody (which excludes others) to Everybody (which includes others).

A wonderful demonstration of this transition from Somebody to Everybody is provided by the Olympics. During the games we see Somebody Training in action: the intense competition of individuals; separation created by 'us against them'; the disappointment of losing; and the elation of winning. But when the games are over, a magical transformation happens. The athletes enter the arena for the grand finale, this time, not as competitors, but as part of the human family. They have dropped their national flags – the flags that separate. Any sense of struggle, fear, anger and upset that went on during the games seems to have dissolved. We are aware of the communion, camaraderie, joy, even bliss that radiates throughout the stadium and into our homes as we watch the spectacle on television. Our hearts swell, and it is hard to hold back the tears at the vision of what life could look like if we were able to elevate ourselves to that level of connection – that level of Everybody-ness – in all that we do.

Few of us know how, which is why there is so much yearning and emptiness in our lives. Thus it is my purpose to help you see the world through the eyes of the Higher Self, enabling your alienation to lessen and the loving essence of who you are to emerge. The pathway to the Higher Self is through the lessons of our Everybody Training.

So let's begin with an Everybody Training truth about connection:

> Connection is made easier when we
> approach other people with the primary
> purpose of making *them* feel better about
> themselves.

The key word in this formula is **them**. The reason most of us are so fearful of approaching others is that, whether we are consciously aware of it or not, we usually approach people with the primary purpose of making *us* feel better about ourselves! Our hesitation about approaching others comes from the awful possibility that, instead of feeling better about ourselves after we make the big move toward connection, we'll end up feeling like a jerk!

'Not me', you say? 'I'm just shy.' Think about it. The basic reasons we are timid about making contact – whether for business, friendship or romance – are that:

- We fear rejection.
- We fear that we are not good enough.
- We fear that we have nothing to say.
- We fear we'll make a fool of ourselves.
- We fear being put down in some way.

When we are afraid, we are not focusing on the other person at all – we are only focusing on ourselves. Our internal voice is not saying 'Perhaps that person is lonely and would like someone to talk to' or 'Perhaps there is a way that I could make that person feel good about himself.' No, it is saying, 'Perhaps she'll think I'm coming on to her' or 'I look really lousy tonight and he'll find me totally unattractive.' We are so worried about the way we appear to that other person, that we cannot 'see' that he or she may be needing something from us – even if it's only the reassurance of a smile.

So we remain on opposite sides of the room, and once again we pass up an opportunity to make a loving connection with another human being. Or we physically connect, but, because of our nervousness, never really *listen* to what the other person is saying or *feel* what the other person is feeling. Hence, in effect, there is no connection at all.

Please note that I am not telling you all this to make you feel badly about yourself – I do understand how lousy so many of us feel about ourselves. I know how much it hurts to feel small and insignificant. I know some of us have been taught, directly or indirectly, that no one really wants to hear what we have to say, or that we are stupid, or that we should be seen and not heard, or whatever. I know how paralyzing these feelings can be. So why am I telling you all this? First, to show you that the Somebody Training question, '**What am I going to get?**', laces all our interactions with the fear of not getting and ultimately, not getting enough. The Everybody Training question, '**What am I going to give?**', introduces a sense of outflow and abundance. To be the 'giver' rather than the 'getter' therefore makes us feel more secure.

Some of you may be feeling, 'Wait a minute! I give and give and give, and get nothing back in return.' I am not suggesting that you be a doormat for hurtful people in your life. On the contrary, we need to walk away from people who treat us unkindly. What I am suggesting is that when we begin to see connection as a **giving** to someone, we can feel more at peace in our attempts to connect with others . . . **whether we are rejected or not.** Of course, rejection never feels good:

it always touches the insecurity within us, no matter
how much confidence we have gained. But it feels
much better when we are not needing something from
the person who is rejecting us – that I can guarantee.
Ultimately, we learn that when we approach someone
lovingly and are treated unkindly, we are learning a
lot about *their* insecurities. **Secure people don't treat
other people unkindly, no matter what the situation**.

John Powell has made the observation that we must
use things and love people.[3] However, when we are
fearful, we are locked into the trap of using people
instead of loving them. This applies equally in all areas
of our lives. People become objects to provide us with
something we need; they do not appear to be human
beings with their own insecurities and their own need
to be loved, just like you and me.

You now see why Everybody Training teaches us to
focus on the giving instead of the getting. As you
continue reading, you will learn how to put this
concept into practice. For now, simply be aware that
our own insecurities make it hard to give. As an exercise, you might want to keep a log of your interactions
with other people, setting up different sections of the
log for romance, friendship and business. Leave a
space to answer the following questions about each:

> Did I approach this person with the
> purpose of getting something from him (or
> her)? Or did I approach this person with the
> purpose of giving something to him (or her)?
> (Something = praise, a job, a compliment, a
> thank you, a date, sex, a sale, a favour, a pat
> on the back, a meal and so on.)
>
> If I approached this person with the sole

purpose of getting something from him (or her), how might I have turned my thinking around to include giving something?

In the beginning, it isn't necessary to do anything with your answers to these questions. **As you become more aware of your actions and intentions, you will automatically become more giving to others**. Be patient with yourself. Becoming a giver may at first be very difficult and uncomfortable. It means that we have to let go of a lot of our earlier training. As we walk into the freedom that human connection allows, we may have to return to our isolation a few times before we can muster enough courage fully to embrace with outstretched arms that world out there. But as we slowly begin to feel better about ourselves, something wonderful begins to happen. The numbness starts to disappear and feelings of empathy and caring come pouring in.

By acknowledging that every 'stranger' in that crowded room would love to feel cared about and has often felt themselves to be a Nobody, just as we have, we are in harmony with them even before we ever say hello. When this happens, we truly understand the truth behind the words 'there are no strangers', and the world doesn't seem so lonely any more.

The Journey Inward to Connection

2

Finding the Warmth

The first time I met Jonathan was at a party. Clearly, he didn't have a problem with connection in most people's terms. He talked to lots of guests and appeared to be having a wonderful time – laughing, touching, listening and so on. One would think he knew all the secrets of successful connection, and on a surface level he did. But, beneath the surface, there was another story to be told.

I next met up with Jonathan when I was invited to sit in on a men's self-help group. It was in the safety of this group, which he'd been attending for six months, that he was able to talk with great poignancy about his many fears and unrelenting loneliness. He said, with tears in his eyes, that he went to parties, met a lot of people, yet usually ended up going home alone. Something within him was not allowing any true connection to occur. His greatest fear was that he would be alone and lonely for the rest of his life.

Hence, despite his successful party techniques,

Jonathan is no better off in terms of his ability to connect authentically than the wallflower in the corner who never has the courage to walk up to someone and say that first hello. Despite the differences in the way they handle their exterior worlds, both are internally experiencing similar kinds of alienation from themselves and others. Let's take a look at what goes on within that prevents successful connection from occurring.

Did you ever ask yourself *why* people reach out to connect with one another? Of course, there are the apparent reasons – to find a mate, to gain new clients, to make new friends and so on. But if we looked a little deeper, we would see a complex web of human emotions that makes us reach out for other reasons. Some form the basis of healthy connection and others of unhealthy connection. Using the model of Somebody Training versus Everybody Training, let's take a deeper look:

Everybody Training Reasons
for Reaching Out

To share our warmth and caring and love; to participate within the human family; to make the world, in our own unique way, a better place for all of us.

versus

Somebody-Based Reasons
for Reaching Out

> To 'fix' something within ourselves – such
> as our low sense of self-esteem, our
> unhealthy dependency and our loneliness.

The difference is dramatic. And the implications are even more so. It stands to reason that when we reach out so that someone can 'fix' us, the results can be disappointing at best and humiliating at worst. We are assured of failure, since

> No one can fix what's broken inside except
> ourselves.

We may find a temporary fix, but, as we all know, temporary fixes always wear off and we find ourselves right back where we started.

Let's take romance as an example (remembering that the same model applies to other areas of our life). Sometimes we dive into romantic relationships in order to mask our neediness. Because relationships based on neediness are only sticking plasters for an inner problem, they are never fulfilling for very long – if ever. Remember what happens to plasters? When you put them on, they feel clean, healthy and secure. In a very short time they get sticky and dirty, and ultimately you have to take them off before the finger gets infected! My own story demonstrates this analogy beautifully.

I met my first husband on my first day at college as my father's car pulled away from the hall of residence. We were married within the year. At the time, I felt very lucky to have found my 'prince' at such an early age. It would take me many years to realize that the prime motivation for my marriage was not love (even though he was a terrific person and I loved him as much as I was capable of loving anyone at the time); rather it was the act of a dependent, frightened and lonely young woman trying to find solace in a substitute parent.

It would also take me many years to realize that, while my marriage allowed me to mask the intense loneliness and fear that constantly lurked beneath the surface, these painful feelings always managed to seep out sideways in the form of anger, jealousy, judgment, unrealistic expectations, feelings of abandonment and emptiness. Hardly a good basis for a healthy relationship. As I mentioned earlier, all the while I thought there was something wrong with *him* which was causing all my painful feelings and unloving behaviour. I was too self-righteous (an obvious sign of insecurity) to notice that I had more than a few issues to work on within myself.

When I ended my marriage after sixteen years, I felt I would have no problem being on my own. After all, I was a big girl. Hence I was not prepared for the anguish that I actually felt – anguish that came from feeling miserably lost and alone in the world. None of it made any sense to me then. On an objective level, I wasn't lost at all. I had diligently learned all the rules for being a Somebody in the world. I had two lovely children, a PhD in psychology, a terrific job, a wonderful circle of friends and no problem getting dates. My outer life was full, but my inner life remained unrelentingly empty. It was only then that I realized that my marriage had served as a sticking plaster. While we remain very good friends, our marriage served to mask unresolved issues lurking since my childhood.

Looking back, I can now identify the feelings I was experiencing – loneliness, low self-esteem, emptiness, dependency, anger and fear – as a form of '**spiritual separation**', a lack of connection with the essence of who I truly was. In the way that I am using the term, spiritual separation has nothing to do with religious belief or its absence. It has to do with a life lived without any connection to the Higher Self, that place within where all separateness disappears and a sense of wholeness appears.

Given our society's priorities, it is not surprising that one can live for years without ever having faced the question, 'Who am I?' In an environment that conditions us to suppress our true selves and conform to the dictates of our parents, peers, religion and society, there is little room for self-discovery and spiritual growth. Denied the knowledge of how to access this place of safety within, we constantly feel a yearning to return home. We believe it must be our parental home that we are yearning for – the one we actually had when we were young (or the one we always longed to have). We try desperately to create a new place of safety by attaching ourselves to someone else – but it never works for very long. Without our primal connection with our selves, true connection with others is impossible. And so the longing persists.

In my case, it was my divorce that set the wheels in motion for my spiritual separation to end and my spiritual connection – that is, connection with my Higher Self – to begin. The truth about my loneliness, childlike dependence and lack of self-esteem was finally out in the open and I could ignore it no longer. I had to acknowledge the fact that my prime motivation for latching on to other people was to keep the unrelenting emptiness at bay. Intuitively, I realized that the only way I could authentically connect, without an ulterior motive, was to acknowledge that the keys to hearth and home lay safely within my being – not in somebody else's. In order to feel this security, I had to 'find myself' – whatever that meant.

I began to force myself to spend time alone, which is not so easy for a lonely and insecure person to do. At first, my thoughts were filled with yearning, fear and anger. I listened for the voice of the Higher Self that I knew lived somewhere inside of me, but was now hidden beneath the many layers of conditioning. My pain reminded me how far I had travelled from the core of my very being.

Sometimes the solitude was terrifying; sometimes it was exhilarating. Sometimes I simply sat clasping my abdomen, feeling that I would explode with the emptiness. Sometimes I was joyful about a new discovery I had made in my ability to enjoy life on my own. I cried a lot; I laughed a lot. I experienced a lot of fear; I experienced a lot of growth. Because I didn't know who I was and what I liked doing, I began experimenting. I read. I went to workshops. I learned how to meditate. I travelled. I forced myself to eat alone in restaurants until I learned to love it. Slowly I began to find the unused parts of myself.

I also made changes in my outer world that went along with the changes I was beginning to feel inside. I let go of any friends who looked at life as an empty experience and sought friends who saw life as a joyous and fulfilling adventure. I took more risks. I learned how to respect who I was and not cave in to peer pressure. I lessened my need for approval from others so that it became easier to like myself. I learned that my life had value, and I participated fully in my job and community.

As I describe in my 'diary' entitled *Losing a Love . . . Finding a Life*, all this growth was not an overnight process; rather it took place minute-by-minute . . . day-by-day . . . week-by-week . . . month-by-month . . . and year-by-year. And with each step, my life kept getting better . . . and better . . . and better. And then came the moment of triumph when I realized that the yearning and fear and anger had been replaced by feelings of contentment, fulfilment and love. While I don't always feel connected with my centre, this sense of wholeness permeates my being most of the time. And for that I feel truly blessed.

Twelve years after my divorce, having discovered how wonderfully a relationship works when emptiness has been replaced by a feeling of self-created fullness, I married again. The neediness that characterized my previous relationships has been replaced with a sense of genuine caring and sharing . . . and love. My experience has taught me that the three biggest barriers to authentic connection – low self-worth, dependency and loneliness – have nothing to do with anyone 'out there'.

> Our barriers to connection have only to do with our inner wounds that need to be self-healed and our inner fears that need to be self-calmed.

As we heal our inner world, our outer world 'miraculously' gets healed as well. Our lives become enriched with fulfilling jobs, supportive friends and loving relationships. We begin to notice the beauty of all those people out there who would welcome our love. And in this wholesome space, loving connections can occur in all areas of our life.

With that in mind, let's look at some inner work that paves the way for successful connections to occur.

> While it is true that we never break totally free from our earlier training, we all can learn to walk *inward* into a far more loving place.

3

I Want You to Like Me

Author and teacher Alan Cohen tells the following story:[1] At the opening session of a human relations workshop he attended, all of the participants were asked to write on a white gummed label something they wanted to tell about themselves to the others in the room. They were then required to stick this little piece of paper on their foreheads and walk around the room reading the messages on everyone else's foreheads. An interesting way of breaking the ice, indeed!

Most of the messages were of the 'I love to travel', 'I like to play squash' and 'I've just left a relationship' variety. But one message stood out in Cohen's mind as the one that said it all – the one that broke through all the *indirect* messages that were being presented. That message was:

I want you to like me.

Metaphorically, we all wear an 'I want you to like me' sticker on our foreheads. Whether we are conscious of it or not (and most of us are not), much of our behaviour – good or bad – is simply part of an *act* that we developed as children in the hope that it would earn us much needed attention and/or approval. Our act probably underwent some modification as the years went by, but the *reason* for the act always remained the same – we want to be liked. In fact,

> We *need* to be liked.

John Powell presents us with a very poignant answer to the question 'Why am I afraid to tell you who I really am?'

> 'I am afraid to tell you who I am, because, if I tell you who I am, you may not like me, and it's all that I have.'[2]

That's a good clue as to why connection is so difficult. Implicit in this answer are the following truths that we consciously or unconsciously hold about ourselves:

> 'I want you to like me. But I don't like me. If you really knew me you wouldn't like me either. Therefore, I'll pretend to be different from what I really am.'

And to make matters worse, the person with whom we are playing this sad little deception is consciously or unconsciously saying to him or herself,

> 'I want you to like me. But I don't like me, and if you really knew me you wouldn't like

me either. So, I'll pretend to be different from what I really am.'

What we are left with is two people **trying** to connect, **wanting** to connect, **yearning** to connect, but who have no way of penetrating each other's masks. It doesn't matter whether these two people are sisters, brothers, parents, children, friends, colleagues, lovers, mates, 'strangers' in the street or some combination of these. The masks are worn by all of us.

We don our masks very early in life. As helpless children, we are dependent on our parents for our physical and emotional survival. Therefore, we live with the terrifying thought that **'If I don't measure up, they might go away!'** Because of our terror, we begin hiding – and ultimately denying – the part of ourselves that could bring disapproval from our parents and, later, our teachers and peers. For example, if we are taught that we must be generous, we disown the part of us that is greedy. If we are taught that we can't be angry, we stifle the rage building within. If we are taught that we must be strong, we hide our tears. If we are taught that we must be physically attractive, we hide the 'flaws' with make-up, deodorant, dyed hair, trendy clothes, cologne, shoelifts and so on.

Consciously or unconsciously, we believe that no one could love us as we truly are. Eventually, we lose all sense of who we really are and our act becomes our identity. What is left is a fearful robot who has long ago forgotten the answer to the question, 'Who am I?'

When we are lost to ourselves, how can we possibly connect meaningfully with someone else?

This alienating pattern changes only when we begin the process of reconditioning ourselves to feel the enormous power and beauty that we truly are.

You might be thinking, 'It certainly sounds like some sort of vicious plot that all of us grow up feeling inferior to some degree or another.' It's really not. It has more to do with a society that truly believes Somebody Training to be a positive thing, a society that doesn't understand how its rules create an inability to love ourselves. Thankfully, we can reverse the process and turn the self-hate into self-love. I've provided some exercises to help you do just that. They are meant to eradicate the false self and convince you that who you are is good enough. Only then can you allow your authentic self to emerge.

I urge you not only to read through these exercises, but to take responsibility for incorporating them into your daily life. Don't cheat yourself out of the joy of a life filled with power and love that comes with improving the way you feel about yourself. Remember . . . the exercises work only if you do![3]

EVERYBODY TRAINING EXERCISES FOR LIKING OURSELVES

Stop trying to be 'perfect'

This is one situation where 'giving up' has to be the healthiest thing you can do for yourself. So breathe a sigh of relief, and rest easy as you stop trying to do the impossible. Understand that the loveliest thing you can do for yourself is to **embrace the beauty of your humanness**.

A good start is to implant the following Everybody Training thought in your mind by simply repeating it at least ten times a day:

> *I am good enough exactly as I am . . . and who I am is a powerful and loving human being who is learning and growing every step of the way.*

I can hear you saying 'Oh, come on! This hardly describes *me*!' On the surface, it doesn't always describe me, either! So what does this statement really mean? It doesn't mean that there aren't unhealthy patterns within us that we wouldn't like to make healthier. It doesn't mean that we are always proud of the way we behave. It doesn't mean that we have learned everything we need to learn about becoming a more loving person. But it does mean that the essence of who we are is wonderful. It also means that every experience in our lives – the good *and* the 'bad' – can enrich us in some way.

We learn that everyone's journey takes a different route. I might get there through years of being a driven perfectionist, you might get there through twenty-five years of a bad marriage, and your friend may get there through illness or alcohol. But from our different experiences, we ultimately can come to the deep understanding that we are all heading in the same direction . . . to the place of love within us all. In any case, the place and the person we are at this very moment is perfectly imperfect indeed!

An article by Linda Weltner entitled 'The Miracle of Imperfection'[4] points out that when we expect perfection in anyone, including ourselves, we are treating that person as if he or she is a machine. (And even machines break down!) When we treat people as machines, we lose our human connections. I don't find it very satisfying going to lunch, to bed, to the movies or to work with 'machines'. I'd rather be with human beings who sometimes make mistakes, get confused, feel insecure, get old, who reach out with their humanity and who touch the humanity inside of me.

> It is through our humanness, not our perfec-
> tion, that the poignant bonds of connection
> are finally formed.

Become an Everybody-Trained parent to yourself

While our parents may or may not have been loving to us as we were growing up, it is important to keep remembering that we are all products of a Somebody Training world. We have all been trained to feel 'not good enough' about ourselves. Part of our inner work now involves providing ourselves with the uncondi-tional loving approval that was unavailable during childhood.

Most of us do just the opposite: we go about our lives pulling ourselves down instead of building ourselves up. The negative internal voice which I call the Chatterbox constantly reminds us of our 'flaws', telling us we should be thinner, smarter, more organ-ized, stronger, richer, prettier. If we are to feel better about ourselves, it is clear that the Chatterbox must be silenced and replaced by a much more loving voice.

A very effective tool that provides this loving voice is the **guided visualization**, which is a closed-eye process that can help you feel better about yourself. One of several uses of the guided visualization is to allow your imagination to create circumstances in your life as you want them to be, rather than as they may be at the present time. As the picture of your ideal life becomes clearer in your head, the more likely you are to make the picture a reality. I've included a powerful visualization for connection, complete with explanation and instructions, in the Appendix. It will be helpful to do this guided visualization before any social or business situation that makes you fearful – it will bolster your self-confidence enormously.

Another effective tool for replacing the Chatterbox is the **affirmation**, which is a form of positive 'inner-talk'. Affirmations are strong positive statements that transmit the message to ourselves, 'I'm really an OK person.' Some examples of 'loving parent' affirmations that are meant to be repeated to yourself are as follows:

> *I am powerful and I am loving.*
> *I have much to give to this world.*
> *I am a person of worth.*
> *I deserve love.*
> *I am a capable person.*
> *My life has meaning.*
> *My life is unfolding perfectly.*
> *There is plenty of time.*

Note that you do not have to believe these affirmations for them to work! The mere saying of them over and over again begins to reprogramme the negative pictures you have of yourself. Set aside at least ten minutes a day to practise your affirmations. Use them every time you notice negative chatter going on in your head. There are many audiotapes available comprised totally of affirmations that you can listen to as you dress, lie in bed in the morning or evening, or drive to work. They help to obliterate the negativity and fill you with confidence. Regular use of affirmations can create remarkable changes in a person's life, and I urge all of you to learn their proper use. I am such a fan of positive affirmations that I have created three 'Inner Talk' CDs to help convince you that you are powerful and loving and have nothing to fear.[5] I have also created a free 25 page affirmation booklet entitled *Why Affirmations are so Powerful!* that you can download from my website (www.susanjeffers.com). Yes, I love affirmations!

To remind you further to be a loving parent to yourself, put signs all over the house and car, in your diary and anywhere you can see them, that contain some version of 'NO SELF-CRITICIZING ALLOWED'. The aim is to catch yourself automatically when you begin putting yourself down. You can also enlist the help of your friends to point out to you how and when you unconsciously put yourself down. (It goes without saying that it is necessary to move away from the put-down artists you call friends who do the criticizing for you!)

Still another way we have of reprogramming ourselves and getting rid of our old critical Chatterbox is to

> *Remove those 'I want you to like me' stickers from our foreheads and, instead, place them where they truly will do the most good . . . on our mirrors!*

I'm speaking literally as well as figuratively. We actually need to *see* the message on the mirror so that our minds, which are usually so busy putting us down, will begin pulling us up. On most occasions when we look into the mirror, our Chatterbox sends us such messages as, I never noticed that wrinkle before', 'My eyes seem terribly puffy', 'My skin looks yukky', and so on. Every time you see something negative in the mirror, switch to something positive. This will help you learn to love the person looking back at you.

It is when we look into the mirror that we usually face our cruellest critic. Nobody can hurt us the way we hurt ourselves. It is important to remind ourselves constantly where our need for approval arises – and where it will end. We must be able to look into that mirror with confidence and approval and be able to say to ourselves with total conviction,

> *'Yes, I really like you. I appreciate the beauty of who you are. I would be proud to be your friend, colleague, mate. I find you a strong and beautiful soul who makes my heart sing.'*

When we finally reach this point in our evolution, it doesn't matter whether someone else likes us or not and we can allow our authentic self to emerge – a first step in creating the bonds of connection.

Figure out your act and begin dropping it

As you can imagine, this is very scary in the beginning, since our sense of what is OK is tied up with our act. But when we finally peel away the layers of who we are not, and get to the core of who we are, we make a thrilling discovery:

> Who we *truly* are is very lovable and very powerful.

It's a guarantee. How can I make that guarantee? Because as we get past all the acts of who we are – the positive and the negative – and finally enter the place of our Higher Self, we touch the part of ourselves that is endowed with an inherent sense of power and love. It is also the place where 'I am you and you are me'. If, in our lives, any of us behave in ways that are powerless and unloving, it's only because we've travelled so far from the essence of who we truly are.

As I explained earlier, when we allow our Higher Selves into our thinking we can also embrace, instead of abhor, the 'lower' part of who we are. That is, we accept the anger, greed, fear and every other emotion that lives within us just as part of being human. With acceptance of all of who we are, we can then safely allow our masks to drop and tell the truth without fear of disapproval. (Can you see the bonds of connection beginning to form?) If someone disapproves, it doesn't matter. At this point, we will finally have approval from the person we have been unsuccessfully trying to impress all these years: not mother, not father, not teacher, not the kids in the neighbourhood – but ourselves.

To peel away the acts that have removed us from our authentic selves, it helps first to identify our 'I want you to like me' style or styles of behaving. Psychiatrist W. W. Broadbent identifies a few:[6]

- **Man's-man style** (I'm absolutely fearless.)
- **Saint style** (Aren't I sweet, smiling, loving and accepting?)

- **Windy style** (Aren't I wonderfully articulate?)
- **Chameleon style** (I'll be anything you want me to be.)
- **Moralizer style** (I am virtuous and righteous and I always do what I 'should' do . . . and so should you!)
- **Frightened-fawn-in-the-forest style** (I am weak and need you to take care of me.)
- **Martyr style** (Oh, what I've done for you and I get nothing in return.)
- **Super-self-sufficient style** (I don't need you. I don't need anyone.)
- **Playing-authentic style** (Look how honest and forthright and authentic I am.)
- **Toilet-bowl syndrome** (Poor, poor me. The whole world is shitting on me!)
- **Red cross nurse style** (Can't you see how giving and nurturing I am?)
- **Guru style** (Look how wise I am.)
- **One-upman style** (See how cleverly I can put anyone down.)
- **Fan style** (Whatever you do, it's great!)
- **Nice-guy style** (How could you help but like such a charming, sweet guy as I am?)
- **Dig me style** (Don't I entertain and amuse you?)

You may be wondering why some of us take on seemingly productive acts and others destructive ones. John Bradshaw believes that the false self can take many forms. But basically we fall into two groups:

1) The 'There is no hope' group, or
2) the 'I'll try harder' group[7]

Those in the 'There is no hope' group behave *less than human* and take on the form of an alcoholic, slob, drug addict, doormat, child-beater and so on. Clearly, this is the group of us that simply gives up, realizing that there is no way to be perfect. Those in the 'I'll try harder' group behave *more than human*, becoming the workaholic, perfectionist, people-pleaser, optimist, life and soul of the party, do-gooder and so on.

I would suggest a third, the 'I'll do anything to belong' group. Those in this group will adopt any behaviour just to fit in. This behaviour could be *less than human or more than human*, depending on the situation. If they are in the company of 'tough guys', the 'I'll do anything to belong' group takes on an 'I am a tough guy' act. If they are in the company of do-gooders, they take on an 'I am doing good' act. Anything to belong! The irony is that, when we twist ourselves in this way, we never have the sense that we truly belong anywhere.

As an exercise, identify as many of your own personal acts as you can. You can turn this into a kind of helpful game if you invite a few caring friends over and spend an evening discussing everyone's favourite acts. Good friends can help point out some you didn't even know you had! Sharing with others is also a great way for us to be honest about what's true for all of us – our need to be liked, and what lengths we will actually go to to make that happen. When it's done in the name of love, this process can be very enlightening.

Note that not all our 'acts', are negative. It is our *motivation* that is important. If we are a 'nice guy' because of the joy of being a giving person, that's great; but if we are a 'nice guy' only because we're desperate to belong, we are unauthentic and immediately prevent true connection from happening. After all, what happens when two actors try to connect? Inevitably, you get a 'performance' that looks like connection and sounds like connection, but isn't the real thing.

Once we discover our various acts for gaining approval, we must remember not to put ourselves down. We discover our act only to empower ourselves. First, we notice: 'Ah, yes. There's Susan doing her pleasing – everyone number again. Obviously, she isn't feeling good about herself right now.' No self-criticism here – only noticing. With this observation, we know it's time to pick up our bag of self-esteem tools and put them into practice. Watching ourselves in this way automatically sets the stage for our ultimately letting go of our fake selves.

Again, understand that the processes of discovering and dropping our acts don't occur overnight. As with all reprogramming activities the change takes place over a lifetime, as we slowly live more and more into our authenticity. It takes courage to drop our act. For example, it takes courage to say no when our act is to be a people-pleaser. It takes courage to say 'Please help me' when our act is to be independent. But with each step we learn to know and like ourselves a little bit more.

Attend a Co-dependency Anonymous (CoDA) meeting

CoDa uses an adapted version of the Twelve Steps associated with Alcoholics Anonymous (AA) to deal with problems of co-dependency. Originally, the term 'co-dependent' was used to describe someone whose life was enmeshed with an alcoholic, but it's now being described as a **disease of lost self-hood**. In a co-dependent personality, the real self is hidden and the false self is adopted to 'fit into' a society that demands unreal behaviour on our parts. (Sound familiar?) Some have described it as a dependency on approval from others as they search for a feeling of safety, love and inner peace.

Co-dependent behaviour is often a natural reaction to a dysfunctional family. And I've come to the realization that, because of our Somebody Training, by definition

We all come from dysfunctional families!

Even if our family appears to be normal and loving, it is important to understand that the whole of society is dysfunctional in its expectations and values. We need only to look around and notice that:

Even for those of us who seem to function beautifully in this world, there is a constant struggle to stop struggling and to live life in spiritual harmony.

So we can all benefit from CoDA (although if you are in therapy, consult your therapist before attending a CoDA meeting – or any group meeting, for that matter). CoDA is not therapy in the common usage of the term. As with all the twelve-step programmes, its members take turns in leading the meetings. There are no fee or registration requirements. Just show up. The groups meet regularly, and in larger communi-

ties, at different locations. If you don't feel comfortable in one group, try another. Remember that it is
common to feel some initial discomfort in any group
of 'strangers'. You will feel more at ease as time goes
by.

Primarily CoDA is a programme of learning how to
share – to connect. It is designed to help you tell the
truth about who you are, to help you take responsibility for your own life without blaming others, to help
you love yourself as you deserve to be loved, and to
help you trust in a higher power (whatever that means
for you). Most importantly, it beautifully demonstrates
the reality that 'there are no strangers'. We are all in
it together, all fearful individuals trying very hard in
our own way to make it in this seemingly hostile world;
all trying to learn how to make the world more peaceful
and loving for ourselves and others.[8]

Try some 'inner child' work

Since so many of our problems of self-esteem and
dependency start when we are young and are carried
with us – consciously or unconsciously – all through
life, we may want to find a way of going back and
correcting the implanted 'errors' in our thinking so
that we can let go of our destructive patterns of behaviour. Inner-child work-shops are a way of getting us
back to where the trouble began and reprogramming
ourselves into a more loving way of seeing ourselves
in this world. Look in your area to see if any such
workshops are available and if they seem right for you.
In addition, more and more books are being written
that deal with healing the inner child. I've suggested
two in the chapter notes.[9]

Plant seeds of self-respect

All of us, at times, behave in ways that take away our
self-respect. One obvious way is drinking too much.
Other instances are less obvious. For example, when
we are dependent personalities, we create 'connec-
tion-killers' that lower our self-respect. These include
anger, judgment, manipulation, impossible expectations, helplessness, envy, jealousy, self-righteousness,
super-independence, lack of commitment and so on.
It is important that, *without blaming ourselves*, we become
observers of what we do to lower our self-respect. And
then it is important to act in a manner that raises it.
Here's the magical formula:

> When you put loving thoughts and behav-
> iour into the world, you plant seeds of self-
> respect. When you put unloving thoughts
> and behaviour into the world, you destroy
> seeds of self-respect.

Simple, isn't it – at least, in principle. Not so simple in
execution. Loving ourselves and others is impossible to
do all the time. Our internal Chatterbox is always there
to introduce fear thoughts that take away our ability to
love. But as we continue on the path towards our Higher
Self, the balance improves – the number of loving acts
increases and the number of unloving acts decreases.

Putting out loving thoughts and behaviour does not
mean that we allow others to walk all over us. In fact,
when we let others walk over us, we are killing our
self-respect.

> Nothing is as unattractive as footprints on
> the face!

When we stand tall and respect who we are, we naturally open our hearts and draw more beautiful people into our lives. Always remember that like attracts like. With open hearts, we draw open hearts into our lives. With closed hearts, we draw closed hearts.

One way to plant seeds of self-respect is to volunteer to work for a charity or cause in which you believe. Nothing does more to create a feeling of self-respect than being a helpful force in this world; the satisfaction can be enormous. Becoming a voluntary worker reduces the self-absorption that creates a sense of isolation, and directs our attention to others – thereby helping us feel more at home in the world.

I suggest you take out a pen and pad and answer the question 'What makes me feel great about myself and what doesn't?' Look at your life and write down how you can systematically begin to root out the seeds of self-destruction and replace them with seeds of self-respect. Give these seeds the time to take root and grow, and soon you will see a beautiful garden that represents the best of who you are.

Again, don't be impatient. **Note every step forward**, no matter how big or small. At some point during each day, take a few minutes to write down all the ways you have added to the light that warms the world. Make a note of every compliment and 'thank you' you utter, every nice thought you think, every time you lend a helping hand, every time you make others feel good about themselves. With each acknowledgment of your own inner beauty, you soothe the hurt within. Only you can create the experience of self-worth for yourself – no one out there can create it for you. And once you've got it, no one can take it away.

4

Healing the Lonely Heart

Loneliness is a feeling that can lead us towards greater exploration of who we truly are and what we have to give to this world, and thus towards authentic connection. Or it can lead to self-destructive actions in our desperate attempt to fill the emptiness inside.

Whether loneliness is enriching or destructive in our lives depends on our willingness to pick up the mirror and look it squarely in the eye. Sometimes this is difficult, because loneliness is too often an emotion we mask from ourselves. There are an amazing number of escape routes which we take to avoid or deny feeling lonely: workaholism, drug addiction, a whirlwind of social activities, hasty marriages, dehumanizing sexual encounters, blasting radios or televisions, living in the past, restlessness and so on. This is understandable; loneliness can be very painful. But when it is hidden, it becomes our master and we are but robots trading our aliveness for imagined safety. When it is out in the open, on the other hand, we become its master and use it as a stepping stone towards greater fulfilment.

Where does all this loneliness come from? Most experts would agree that loneliness is felt in infancy, as we begin to experience our own separateness. Experts do not agree, however, as to why it persists. Their observations revolve around three categories:

1) physical separation
2) emotional separation
3) spiritual separation.

PHYSICAL SEPARATION

There is very little sense of permanence or continuity in today's world. By definition, the technological society is an age that creates separation and isolation. It allows an enormous amount of physical mobility, and, as a result, family members are often scattered all over the country, even the world. The divorce rate is higher than it has ever been, leaving people torn apart from the security of the family unit. Society also allows tremendous job mobility, so that we are constantly facing new challenges and new colleagues. Some even work at home – alone – with the 'company' of their computer.

As a result, life requires many goodbyes to that which is familiar as we make our move from place to place, job to job, situation to situation, house to house, and person to person. Hence, some of our loneliness logically comes from our feeling of having no roots, no community. In fact, it is a tribute to our adaptability that we human beings cope as well as we do.

A second type of physical separation results from

the fact that so many people are shy about inviting people into their lives. As a result, they find themselves without companionship. Lots of people complain that they never meet people or get invited out anywhere, and there they sit, wondering why they are so alone. To me it is clear why they are alone. It is because they're not making an effort to reach out to other people; instead, they are hoping and praying that someone will reach out to them. And that's not the way the world usually works.

> When we depend on the world to invite us in, we create a situation where we are always on the outside looking in, yearning to be a part of the warmth that lies in someone else's heart.

A third type of physical separation is created by our alienation from nature. So many of us are oblivious to the destructive consequences of our actions upon the very thing that gives us life. Our abuse of our planet reflects our loss of self. People are now becoming much more concerned about the environment. Along with this concern comes an observable shift from Somebody Training separateness to Everybody Training togetherness. In the pulling together for a common good, we begin to taste the deliciousness of what 'oneness' on the planet could feel like. As we come to feel a sense of global community, much of our feeling of alienation will be replaced by a feeling of belonging.

EMOTIONAL SEPARATION

Psychologist Ira Tanner suggests it is not physical but emotional separation from people that creates loneliness.[1] It was a great revelation to him in his marriage and family practice to find that **the most intense loneliness is found within a home in which there is no communication**. While we may have the physical closeness of a family, silent dinners and walled-off hearts between family members can create an agonizing sense of loneliness.

Loneliness is often the result of a closed heart. Our fear of being hurt, rejected or judged keeps us frozen in our loneliness. We are not able to open our hearts enough to allow in the warmth of others which would melt the pain we feel inside. We blame someone *out there* for our isolation, not realizing that it is our internal walls, not the actions of others, that are responsible for our pain.

In that place of pain and blame, we become psychologically numb to the feelings of others. We can't feel *their* pain. We can't feel *their* fear. We can't feel *their* loneliness. That is, we can feel no empathy – which is a great glue for connection! When we feel empathy, the walls come tumbling down and what was once *me versus you* becomes *us together*. When we let go of the fear and pain and open ourselves to others, much of the loneliness disappears.

Another reason for our loneliness is the loss of our authentic self as we struggle to conform to society's standards. No wonder we are lonely; when we look inside, it feels like there's nobody home. No wonder we attach ourselves on to someone 'out there' to move in with, literally and figuratively. This is only our desperate attempt to find a place where there really is someone at home.

SPIRITUAL SEPARATION

Spiritual separation has to do with our loss of connection with our Higher Self. Whether we believe in God or not, it is critical that we develop a strong inner spiritual connection, a deep, abiding sense of our own inner power and integrity. When we are not on that path towards inner connection, we experience a heart aching to be healed. And it is healed not by the actions that our Somebody Training asks us to take, but rather by the actions that our Everybody Training asks us to take.

> Our heart is healed only through loving, caring, opening, sharing, helping, giving, feeling, embracing and warming the world with our love.

As you can see, the reasons for our loneliness are varied and so are the many things we can do to begin filling the emptiness we feel inside. Let me remind you once again that this is a step-by-step process. It doesn't happen in one giant leap. Have patience and let a sense of inner peace and fulfilment unfold ... all in its own time.

'FILLING THE EMPTINESS' EXERCISES

Learn the fullness of solitude

In order to handle our loneliness effectively, it is critical that we learn how to be comfortable with solitude. Many of us are not, even if we live alone. The minute we walk in the door, we look to the blare of the radio or television to give us the sense that we are not really alone. Or we pick up the telephone to connect us with a feeling of safety. We avoid being alone for the obvious reason that it can be very painful. And it is this avoidance that keeps us from learning how to feel full in the midst of solitude. What can you do to change the pattern?

a) Take some time to sit in silence
Whenever you have the addictive need to turn on the radio or television or call a friend, simply stop yourself, and let the feelings under the emptiness come up. The real enemy is not the loneliness, but the **avoidance of loneliness**.

b) Allow part of your mind to become the observer of what is going on
That means, watch yourself sitting there experiencing whatever emotions come up. 'Oh, there's Susan feeling lonely again.' What happens when you do this is that you get to see that **it is only one part of you that is lonely, not all of you**. As an illustration, when you began the exercise there was only

| Lonely me |

at which point you felt trapped in the middle of the loneliness. Then, when you became the observer, the situation became . . .

| Lonely me | | Me watching lonely me |

Already you are less lonely, as there are now two of you! What you've done is put a little wedge into that sense of being trapped in your isolation. Taking this step distances us from painful feelings so that we are not consumed by them. We learn that we are *more* than 'lonely me' (or any other emotion we are feeling). Now, as you sit there watching the feelings come up you can take it a step further.

c) Jot your thoughts down on a piece of paper
Writing really helps ease your pain and clarify your thoughts. Keep your notes, being sure to date each one. Given enough time, you will be able to arrange them in chronological order and have the satisfaction of reviewing the immense amount of growth you have attained.

d) Start with a set amount of time for which you are going to sit in silence, and gradually increase it
At the beginning, you may want to sit on your own for only five minutes. The amount of time doesn't matter. As in all human growth activities, it is important to begin where you are. Trying to do too much at one time is a self-defeating mechanism that guarantees failure. Each day slowly increase your time alone, until you feel comfortable just sitting there writing down your thoughts for at least half an hour – or more, if you so choose.

e) To comfort yourself, remember why the feeling of loneliness has come up
The loneliness is there simply because you are giving up your traditional escapes and support systems. You are moving your life support from *outer* to *inner*, and

for a while it will feel as though support is nowhere to be found. It may feel a bit like withdrawal symptoms, whether from a drug, a schedule or an attitude. You're on your own without anaesthesia, and that can be very scary and painful at first. Just go with it.

f) When your allotted time is up, notice that you handled any feelings that came up
As soon as you see that you won't die from your loneliness (and you won't) you'll say, 'Great – I handled that! I can handle it again.'

g) Plan the next time for sitting with your solitude
It is something that needs to be repeated incrementally and systematically. It is a reconditioning process, and as such it takes time to transform the experience from pain to power. Believe it or not, as you make this 'loneliness' activity part of your routine,

> The day will come when you will sit there and notice that loneliness doesn't come up any more.

You will have faced that inner demon and realized that you were stronger than it was. That in itself is incredibly empowering. If you follow this process, you will be well on your way to discovering the joy of solitude.

Create some nurturing alone-time activities at home
Most of us don't allow ourselves any time to read a book at our leisure, meditate, take a long hot bath, listen to inspiring tapes, cook a wonderful meal just

for ourselves (if we like to cook), light the candles and enjoy the peace and solitude. It is imperative that we begin to . . .

> Slow down and listen to 'the still small voice within' that connects us all.

To make these times alone even more pleasurable, **prepare for them, look forward to them and make them a choice instead of a penance!**

If you have children, and rarely find yourself with the luxury of an empty house or free time, get hold of a babysitter or ask a friend to look after your children so you can have some solitude at regular intervals. If you are married or if you have a flat-mate, take advantage of those times when they are off doing something on their own. There is always a way to create a little piece of solitude in our busy lives.

Make this date with yourself a priority. An invitation from a friend coinciding with time you'd planned to spend alone may seem very tempting, especially at the beginning when spending time alone may still feel odd; but remember that learning how to be alone is an important step in learning to connect. Explain to your friend, 'I have a very important date – with myself.'

There was a point in my life, between marriages, when I made it a practice not to accept any invitations between Friday night and Sunday night. And for me, Saturday night was *not* the loneliest night in the week, as the old song of my youth suggests – it became the richest!

> Constant activity in the outside world without the balance of inner activity contributes to

our loneliness. We end up separating
ourselves from the very thing that gives us
peace.

Feeling at ease on your own takes some time. Eventually
you will notice that, slowly but surely, the dread is
being replaced by a feeling of happy anticipation.

Make your home a healing retreat

Take a very long look at the place that you call home.
Does it represent the best in you? Does it give you a
feeling of peace? Does it symbolize your love for yourself?

For so many people, the home they live in is a reflection of the emptiness they feel inside. For example, I
have been in the homes of men and women who are
divorced and it was hard to believe the sense of separation rather than connection that pervaded the space.
One man had been divorced for four years, yet boxes
from his move out of his marital home still cluttered
the living room and bedroom. Who would ever want
to come home to such reminders of endings instead
of new beginnings?

Others live in homes that are far beneath the stan-
dard of what they could enjoy. They claim to be waiting
for someone to come along and then they'll fix up
the place or move somewhere better. What a waste!
They could be surrounding themselves with symbols
of self-love right now! Why wait? Create a home that
you look forward to coming back to. It doesn't require
a lot of money to do that. It requires creativity and
self-respect.

If you have flat-mates who don't share your desire
to improve your home, choose one room, perhaps

your bedroom, to make your sanctuary. Or find a new flatmate. If you have children who constantly invade your privacy, there is usually a little corner of the house that you can call your own. We all need a little refuge from those people or things that demand a part of us. We need to create a place of peace where we can put ourselves back together again when we start feeling fragmented in a world of stress.

Do things outside the house by yourself

The world can be a friendly place, or it can be hostile. The critical factor is our attitude. If we think the world will treat us badly we close our doors, thus plunging ourselves into darkness. If we think the world will embrace us lovingly, we open our doors and step into a world filled with enlightening experiences.

Here are a few activities that I found very valuable in my journey to wholeness:

a) Acclimatize yourself to eating alone in restaurants
At the beginning this can feel very uncomfortable, particularly for women. This is because we have been told that women are not treated well if they eat alone in a restaurant. But any such restaurant should simply lose you as a customer! However, I have *never* been treated badly when eating alone in a restaurant – and I eat out alone all over the world!

During the years I was single, I often ate out alone; and now when I am on a lecture tour, I often eat out alone. And I love it. What do I do? I people-watch, I think, I write, I read, and I truly dine. I don't rush. Sometimes I linger longer on my own than I would with friends or family. It doesn't have to be an expensive restaurant. Good food, a quiet place and friendly service are what you want. Despite any uncomfortable feelings at the outset, the experience of eating out alone will become one that you find very nourishing, in more ways than one.

b) Take short trips to the sea or countryside on your own
One of my favourite activities when I was single was to take long weekend trips to the beach. I would rent a little beach house that belonged to a hotel, bring a stack of books and talk to no one, just enjoying the peace for the entire time. To enhance the feeling of solitude, I always went there in the dead of winter when everything was deserted. I would walk alone on the beach, all bundled up, and at times I felt myself profoundly connected to the entire universe. There were moments when I actually 'felt' the presence of God all around me. Some of the most powerful experiences in my life happened during these times alone. They provided me with some stunningly beautiful insights about life and growth. Yes, at times, it was scary and lonely. But the rewards were monumental.

A lovely book that describes this kind of experience is *A Gift from the Sea* by Anne Morrow Lindbergh, written at a time when women did not have the choices they have today. In that sense it is rather dated, but its message still applies. Lindbergh would leave her five children and husband to go off to a deserted island by herself for a few weeks each year. She says that the parting was the most painful of all – like an amputation. Yet the rewards made up for it. She said, 'Life rushes back into the void, richer, more vivid, fuller than before. It is as if in parting one did actually lose an arm. And then, like the star-fish, one grows it anew; one is whole again, complete and round – more whole even than before, when the other people had pieces of one.'[2]

Yes, nature can present us with our most sublime moments. As I look back on my life, I realize that the key turning points in my quest for wholeness all occurred when I created moments for myself in quiet places – on the beach, on a mountaintop or looking up at the stars. While I have always chosen big city living, my husband and I occasionally escape to a place of great natural beauty that provides more solitude.

c) Travel 'alone' with a tour group of people with similar interests

I can hear the groans as images of tour buses and tourists with cameras around their necks cross before your eyes. Yes, that's what the tour groups look like! But there is more to them than meets the eye.

When I was between my marriages I wanted to travel, but I didn't want to be all alone in exotic new lands where I didn't speak the language. So I'd find special-interest tours that were very reasonable in price and very wonderful in their possibilities for self-growth. For example, I travelled with a group of meditators to Egypt and a group of health professionals to Cuba.

I purposely did not invite a friend on these trips, because I knew that if I did I would not reach out to others the way I would if I were on my own. Also, a companion wouldn't have allowed the time alone that I relished. At many points in our tour-directed day I would drop out and go exploring on my own, and as a result I had some incredible experiences. Yet the group was always available, a great consolation in a place where the language and customs were alien to me.

The reason I emphasize special-interest tours is that common interests offer an immediate point of connection. Also, these tours usually take one off the well-beaten path of regular tours into areas that might be more of interest to you. For example, when I went to India with a Jain monk and some of his disciples, I was able to see magical parts of the Indian culture that I would never have experienced on a regular tour. Special-interest group tours involving art, music, geology or almost any interest abound. Start at a local travel bureau, ask colleagues, buy travel magazines and so on. But before embarking on such an adventure, check out the people who are organizing the tour. Even better, ask to talk to someone who has already made a trip with them.

And remember this: because we all have a fear of the unknown (and travel is definitely an unknown), your body and mind may create considerable resistance to such a trip. For example, I often found myself with flu a week before a scheduled trip. I would simply tell my body, 'Even if you have to be driven to the airport in an ambulance, you are going on this trip.' I always made it to the airport!

Once I got there, I would look at the congregating group and decide that they were all boring and horrible and I would absolutely hate the trip! Of course, I ended up loving most of them and feeling very sad on the last night at the prospect of saying our goodbyes. Tours have an intensity that creates a very strong bonding with people. I carry with me today many wonderful memories of these extraordinary trips into the unknown.

Learn the healing power of meditation

Meditation is a wonderful way of connecting with the self. There are various forms – for example, Zen, Tibetan and transcendental – all of which are well worth your investigation. An enormous number of books have been written on the subject, and there will probably be classes that you can attend in your area. The purpose of meditation is to quiet the chatter in the mind and transcend to a realm of peace.

In its effort to calm us down, meditation teaches us about breathing. Most of us are shallow breathers, yet it is through deeper breathing that we become relaxed and open to taking in the beauty around us. Proper breathing allows the fullness of inner and outer flow, enabling us to see our connectedness with everything that exists. Take a deep breath right now, and notice how it relaxes you.

Meditation also allows us to see the bigger picture. When the mind is cluttered, we only see ourselves as fragmented and tired human beings. When the mind is at peace, we see ourselves floating in a sea of harmony. In life, we must strive for a balance between solitude and involvement. In fact, the secret of handling the stress that is a natural part of most of our lives lies in the moments when we return to the peace of the Higher Self. It is here that we often find answers to pressing problems. As theologian Nouwen so beautifully says, 'It is in solitude that we discover that being is more important than having, and that we are worth more than the result of our efforts. In solitude, we discover that our life is not a possession to be defended, but a gift to be shared.'[3] As you learn that your life is a gift to be shared, you can feel more at ease about inviting other people into your life.

Make the first move

As I mentioned earlier in this chapter, many of us lament the fact that we are often alone. We live with the illusion that there is no one out there to fill the empty spaces. The truth is,

> There really is *never* a need to be alone if you don't want to be.

There are many people out there who would joyfully share our lives. We just have to invite them in. Don't expect them to invite you into their world. They may or they may not. If they do, that's icing on the cake. But it's really up to you.

- Invite someone to have lunch or dinner or go to a movie with you. **Don't expect him or her to invite you**.
- Knock on your neighbours' door and invite them in for a cup of coffee. If they're not at home, leave them a note to call on you. **Don't expect them to invite you**.
- Think about what you love to do and take some classes that revolve around these activities. Invite someone in the class to an activity that is related to this particular shared interest. **Don't expect him or her to invite you**.
- After a weekend workshop, you make the suggestion that everyone gets together at your house for a reunion. **Don't expect them to invite you**.

See yourself at the centre of your own universe into which you want to invite others. Always take the responsibility for taking the first move – and the second and third and fourth, if necessary. I always keep in mind two quotes which I heard many years ago. Put them both wherever they will serve as a constant reminder:

Be the host in life, not the guest.
and
Don't warm yourself by the fire; be the
one to light it!

This doesn't mean that you won't ever be invited to share activities with others; of course you will. Nor does it mean that you can't sometimes just sit there and be the recipient of someone else's warmth; of course you can. The point is **always to be responsible for your own good time**.

In line with being the host in life, and not the guest, you can see how there is never an excuse for being alone on your birthday or Christmas or New Year's Eve or whatever – not when you are creating the party! Once again, notice the control this puts in your hands, not in someone else's. Extend the hand of friendship to many people, so that if a few disappoint you there are always others. There is a wonderful old adage, 'Have at least eight friends. If you need something, seven of them will be busy!' Remember, there is no shortage of potential friends. There are probably only a few million people in your immediate area that would greatly welcome your companionship! If you live in a small town the numbers may be fewer, but the principle is the same. The chapters to come contain some helpful tools to help you push through the fear of making those first moves.

Join a special-interest group

When my husband and I moved to Los Angeles, we knew very few people there. Since so much of what I do professionally and personally revolves around the spiritual journey, I was interested in finding a like-minded group of people with whom to learn and grow. One day, I heard of The Inside Edge,[4] a group that meets for breakfast once a week, during which guest speakers share their ideas about bringing the values of love and caring into all life's activities. There were also many other 'Edge' activities, such as a men's group, a business group, a writers' group, a women's group and a dance group, and many social events as well. It sounded perfect – and it was. My husband and I joined, and in a very short time we felt 'connected' to the other 150 like-minded people that comprised the group.

But this feeling of connection did not happen in an instant. In fact, the first few times my husband and I attended the breakfast meetings, we felt very much like outsiders looking in. But as we actively participated and volunteered in the activities we began to get a wonderful sense of belonging: a warmer group of people would be hard to find, yet it was our *involvement* in the group that created our positive feelings. An acquaintance whom I encouraged to join complained, on the other hand, that no one ever included her in anything. I explained that it isn't about 'being included in' anything – it's about extending yourself outward. Nevertheless she still kept waiting for the group to 'give' her something. She never understood that the 'law of getting' is a direct result of the 'law of giving'. True to form, she soon began finding fault with everyone and everything around her – just as she did in life outside the group. Eventually, of course, she dropped out, thereby missing an opportunity to spend time with lots of interesting people.

There are many types of group you can join – political, religious, sports, spiritual, art, charitable, nature, environmental groups and so on. When you join a special-interest group of any kind, become part of the group by **volunteering, inviting, creating, caring, sharing, giving and loving**. You can then carry this principle of involvement out to the world at large, knowing that

> It is your involvement with the world that makes you feel you truly belong.

Given all that we can do to fill the empty space created by our loneliness, I believe that even those who have learned to be comfortable within themselves and comfortable reaching out to others still experience a degree of loneliness in the depth of their being – something beyond the everyday loneliness of wanting to have someone to go to the movies with. I included the following poem in *Losing a Love . . . Finding a Life*[5]

> My life is beautiful,
> I have it all . . .
> But even in the sunshine,
> One has to cry sometimes.

As I look back to the time I wrote those words, I realize I was talking about the tears of loneliness . . . the kind of cosmic loneliness that comes from the realization of the awesome vastness of the universe and our inability to understand it all. Once we have connected with ourselves, we can be at peace with this kind of loneliness, and recognize it as a beautiful part of the human experience that actually enhances our life. Loneliness can be beautiful when it keeps us moving upwards to greater heights of awareness: when it pulls us forward to learn, to seek, to grow. As long as we use it as a tool for self-discovery, loneliness has magical results. Knowing that it is a call forward, we should not be upset at its presence in our lives. We should just heed its call and ask ourselves how we can move forward into wholeness and love. There is nothing wrong with us when we feel our loneliness. We are not misfits or losers. We are incurably and wonderfully human.

The Journey Outward to Connection

That First Hello: The Essentials of Connection

Imagine yourself standing at the door of an unfamiliar room, facing a room full of 'strangers' and feeling very nervous indeed. The occasion could be purely social or in some way related to business. As you stand there feeling like the outsider looking in, the voice of the internal (and eternal!) Chatterbox is most likely telling you some version of the following:

> I can't see a soul that I know. They all look as if they know each other. I hope someone will talk to me. I'm overdressed. I look fat. Maybe I'd better go and comb my hair. I feel so nervous. I hope I don't have to shake hands with anyone . . . my palms are all sweaty. I feel so lost. Everyone else seems to be so much at their ease. I wish I could leave.

Even if your Chatterbox is on good behaviour and remaining mercifully quiet, you still can't ignore the quickened heartbeat, the churning stomach, or however else your nervousness makes itself felt.

How can we overcome these feelings of discomfort? Can we ever learn to look into a room full of people and simply decide to have a wonderful time connecting with everyone we meet? Or, for that matter, is it possible to approach *all* situations – whether involving one person or one thousand – knowing that there is nothing to fear? The answer is a definite *yes!* Many basic tools and concepts are available to make us feel more comfortable in that metaphorical crowded room (job interview, blind date or introduction to your future mother-in-law).

But first, let's review some of the differences between Somebody Training and Everybody Training.

Somebody Training teaches us to . . .	**Everybody Training teaches us to . . .**
Work on what's outside	Work on what's inside
See how much we can get	See how much we can give
Develop a winning act	Discover the authentic self
Ignore the Higher Self	Act from the Higher Self
Control the actions and reactions of others	Control our own actions and reactions

It is obvious that any tools and concepts of connection that derive from Somebody Training have a different focus from those that derive from Everybody Training. Most techniques featured in magazines and in many self-help books are of the Somebody Training variety. They offer help, but only on a very superficial level. The reason for this is that by definition:

> Any tool coming from our Somebody Training is inherently a tool of separation rather than one of connection.

Somebody Training techniques will always teach us in some way about competition and game playing, about getting something from someone else, and about masking who we truly are. So ultimately they serve to increase fear rather than diminish it. Somebody Training techniques would include dressing to kill; playing it cool; not appearing too anxious; impressing everyone with your money, success or chest size; acting coy; acting 'manly'; acting with bravado; acting; acting; and acting! God forbid that anyone should see us as we truly are!

A recent magazine article telling readers how to make a great impression offered such tips as using a breath mint, keeping an expensive pen in your pocket or bag, wearing expensive shoes and not wearing too much make-up. Hardly tips to build one's confidence! In our society, tips like these may indeed help to create just the kind of initial impression you are looking for. There are a few problems, however.

Problem no. 1 is that the message to our conscious and subconscious mind is *always*, 'You're not good enough the way you truly are and if you don't do something to cover up all those flaws, you won't be acceptable to anyone!' Subtly or not so subtly, we're being told that our genuine selves are not attractive and that we need external 'props' to make the grade. You may argue, 'I don't care about the subconscious message – I need help, and if these techniques work, I'll try them.' This leads us to problem no. 2.

Problem no. 2 is that Somebody Training techniques work only temporarily. They never address the root cause of your fears. What happens beyond that first hello? You're still the 'you' who doesn't feel good enough. You still stand nervously on guard for fear that the 'real' you may come seeping out – hardly a good basis for authentic connection! In fact, many people begin their relationship, date, marry and live the rest of their life standing guard at the door of their authentic self for fear that who they really are is simply not good enough. And if their partner ever found out who they really are, they'd probably leave. So many people are afraid of 'being found out', and this is why.

Let's move on to some techniques of the Everybody Training variety and see how they differ. Remember the original scenario. There you are standing in an unfamiliar room full of 'strangers', and, despite the breath mint and the expensive shoes, feeling very nervous indeed. The negative internal Chatterbox is blabbering away, evaporating every ounce of confidence that you may have mustered. It's time for step no. 1.

1) Say 'Stop!' to the Chatterbox!

That powerful little word is a shortened version of the following:

> *Stop! I'm sick and tired of this and I won't take it any more! I'm replacing you with a voice that respects who I am!*

You will automatically experience a moment of blessed silence within your head. That's the moment quickly to implement step no. 2.

2) Replace the negativity of the Chatterbox with the self-caring talk that comes from the Higher Self

Here is a perfect place and time to use our affirmations, which serve to remind us of our worth. So after telling our Chatterbox to STOP, we begin repeating to ourselves at least ten times in quick succession such positive statements as . . .

> *I am a pleasure to know.*
> *I am proud of who I am.*
> *I am a lovable person.*
> *I have much to give.*
> *I bring light wherever I go.*

Again, the mere saying of these words will begin to make you feel better about yourself and your situation. Remember that you don't have to believe affirmations in order for them to work. Your subconscious mind will absorb them, and that is the most important thing. As you repeat the affirmations, you will notice that you are standing a little taller and feeling a bit calmer. Trust me on this one!

You're then ready to move into the room and focus on a person or a group of people with whom you would like to connect. It is now time for step no. 3.

3) Assure yourself that, no matter what response you get from anyone you meet, you are a worthwhile person!

Read this one again: it is a very important clue as to why we are so afraid to approach another person. We assume that our worth is tied up in the way other people – even so-called 'strangers' – treat us. This simply is not true. Your worth depends on what *you* think of you – and of course, that's part of the problem. Repeat the following statement:

> *No matter how anyone reacts to me,*
> *I know I am a worthwhile person.*

The implication of this statement is profound! Think about it. It means that you're not going to let anyone else determine your worth; it means that the only person in charge of how you feel about yourself is *you*; it means that you are breaking your need-for-approval-from-others habit which has run you for too long; it means that you are silencing the Chatterbox and letting your Higher Self determine your personal worth. A pretty powerful statement, I would say!

4) Walk up and greet the person you are interested in getting to know

I use the word 'greet' purposely as it describes exactly what you want to do. My trusty thesaurus offers the following synonyms for 'greet': 'acknowledge, salute, welcome, hail, receive'. Translated into the kind of words that come from the Higher Self, this means:

> *I acknowledge your presence.*
> *I salute our humanness.*

> *I welcome what you have to offer this world.*
> *I hail the beauty in you.*
> *I receive you with a loving heart.*

In case this all sounds very bizarre, remember that this is Higher Self language – a far different cry from the Chatterbox which would be saying:

> *I want him (or her) to acknowledge my presence.*
> *I want him to salute my humanness.*
> *I want him to acknowledge what I have to offer this world.*
> *I want him to hail the beauty within me.*
> *I want him to receive me with a loving heart.*

This kind of thinking brings terror into our hearts. What if no one does any of the above? Remember, there is never a guarantee that you will get the results you are seeking. The only guaranteed way of getting results that empower instead of destroy is to imprint in your mind your Higher Self message that 'No matter how anyone speaks to me, I am a worthwhile person. My approval depends on no one else.'

Remember that we *never* have control over other people. But we do have control over what *we* think and do in this world. And it is far more nourishing to 'think and do' in the language of self-love and self-respect which comes from Everybody Training techniques.

To strengthen your resolve when you approach another person *in a caring manner* and are fearful they will treat you badly, remember:

> Whatever the situation, the more hurtfully
> or obnoxiously a person ever acts towards

you, the smaller he (or she) feels inside, the more out of touch he is with his own inherent beauty, and the more psychologically numb he is to the feelings of other people. His 'act' of superiority is inevitably his attempt to hide his own humiliating lack of self-worth.

Hang this paragraph on your wall if you have to. Everyone has their out-of-sorts moments, of course, but, generally speaking, anyone who is in touch with their self-worth acts in a kind manner to everyone around him or her.

Now that you are standing before him (or her), what then?

5) Look him (or her) in the eye while silently projecting caring thoughts

In one of my workshops, I use an Everybody Training connection exercise which according to students has helped them break down their discomfort in all manner of social and business encounters. While it is in itself an artificial situation, I will show you later how to apply the general principles in your everyday activities.

First, I ask everyone in the room, all 'strangers' to each other up until now, to find a partner and stand facing one another. (It's at this point that I usually lose one person to the rest room – his or her fear is just too great!) When the rest of the class members, however reluctantly, have all found a partner, I give them the following instructions: 'Look into your partner's eyes. No smiling and no talking allowed. And as you do this, I want you silently to project the following thought:

> *This is a person just like me . . . a human being*
> *with feelings . . . who wants to connect . . . who*
> *wants to be liked . . . who has also faced the pain*
> *of rejection at times . . . and who is just as nervous*
> *as I am.'*

As they are projecting this Everybody Training thought, I remind them again to look into each other's eyes and just *be*. Nothing to do, nothing to say . . . just to *be*! Sounds easy, right? Wrong! It is amazing how difficult it is for someone to do this part of the exercise. Many find the need to smile or joke or talk. To look into another person's eyes and just *be* is very threatening.

If their Chatterbox is rearing its nasty little head and offering such unhelpful statements as 'I wish I had put on more eye make-up today', I tell them just to notice these thoughts, let them go, and concentrate on projecting the Everybody Training thoughts I was giving them. I remind them that connection truly begins telepathically. The thoughts we project set the stage for much of what will happen later.

After a few moments, I say: 'Now I'd like you to smile while still maintaining eye contact. And with your smile, silently project the following thought to your partner:

> *I'd really like to get to know you. I'd like to share*
> *the best of who I am with the best of who you are.*
> *I'd like to support you in feeling great about your-*
> *self. I'd like to be your friend. I appreciate the*
> *essence of who you are.'*

After a few more moments they are instructed as follows: 'Now I'd like you to hug each other, really sharing your warmth with your partner's and taking in the warmth he has to offer you. Feel yourself melting into the hug, truly relaxing into each other's warmth, and silently project the following thought:

> *I give you warmth and comfort as I take in the*
> *warmth and comfort you give to me.'*

And finally, after a few moments, I give them the signal to break apart and thank each other for being their partner.

There is a definite sense of relief in the room as they begin to feel, 'Phew, I'm glad that's over.' But the relief turns to discomfort again as I quickly tell them to pick another partner. I hear a few groans, but they comply. I repeat this process again a minimum of six times, sometimes with partners of the same sex and sometimes with partners of the opposite sex. And, lo and behold, with each change of partners the tension in the room noticeably diminishes.

When the process is over and they return to their seats, it is interesting to notice the changed energy of everyone in the class (except of course, for the fearful person who is just returning from the rest room). Their initial unease has transformed itself into joyful familiarity. Everyone is laughing and chatting to their neighbour. **A sense of connection has permeated the room**.

I point out to them the contrast between this scene and the earlier one as they began filtering into the room before the class began. One by one they entered

the room, looked around sheepishly, and then t...
a seat as far away from everyone else as possible. As
more and more people came into the room, they had
no choice but to sit next to one another. And that is
all they did . . . they sat! Tension and unease were
clearly in the air. Except for a few whispers between
those who had brought along a friend, not a word was
spoken.

And, now, after the connection exercise, I have
trouble restoring quiet. They are so busy comparing
notes with one another. When they have finally calmed
down, I go around the room asking everyone to share
the thoughts they had as they were going through the
exercise. Here are a few of the responses:

- In the beginning I wanted to disappear. And then
  it got easier.
- It was hard to just 'be'. I had to giggle, make a
  joke.
- I find with glasses I feel detached. Maybe they are
  a barrier.
- You certainly feel closer to everyone.
- The smile eased the situation. It felt more comfortable.
- I thought, 'Oh, God, I wish I didn't have this
  spot.' I really felt self-conscious.
- It got easier with practice. I was really nervous to
  begin with, but by the end of the process I even
  looked forward to my next partner.
- I was so caught up in my own unease that I noticed
  it was hard to get into the other person.
- After about thirty seconds, amazing things started
  to happen. I fell in love at least three times!
- I enjoyed watching people become more

as I was more comfortable with
e me a powerful feeling.

fascinating to me to watch the varied
my students move through the process.
As I ___ earlier, without practice it is very difficult
for people to look each other in the eyes without
smiling or talking. The discomfort of just 'being' is
enormous. Most of the class feel a need to *do* something – such as to smile, giggle, make a joke, utter a
sexy remark or tell their partner that he (or she) has
pretty eyes. Even the most outgoing among us have
some difficulty with eyeball-to-eyeball contact.

And then there are the hugs. Some really get in there
with their softness and warmth. Others are so rigid that
no warmth is allowed out – and so, sadly, none is allowed
in. Men find it extremely difficult to hug other men,
so you hear a lot of back-slapping and jokes. It's really
hard for them to show genuine affection without being
a bit 'manly' about it. (I'll discuss this in Chapter 8.)

As already stated, this Connection Exercise is artificial, yet its principles can work with anyone, any time
and any place.

Since readers will not have had the benefit of practising the Everybody Training Connection Exercise in
one of my classes, I've come up with the following
plan for you to follow which will give similar results.
First, as you walk down the street, or shop, or engage
in any activity where there are people around you,
start really 'seeing' other people as you have possibly
never seen them before. We usually see others through
Somebody Training vision. Hence, what ordinarily goes
through our minds are thoughts from the Lower Self
like these:

- 'Ugh, what a lot of make-up! Makes her look grotesque!'
- 'She'd be beautiful if she didn't have such a big nose.'
- 'Isn't he ugly! Who ever would want to go out with him?'
- 'She's a sweetie! I'd love to take her home with me.'
- 'He's really rude to the waiter. What a jerk!'
- 'She's such a slob. Why doesn't she make herself more presentable?'

And so on . . .

It is now time to change the thoughts you project by picking up an Everybody Training script, one written by the Higher Self. This script is very easy to memorize since it consists of just one line. Now, as you once again find yourself in the midst of humanity, silently say to yourself as you look at *everyone* around you:

I greet the light in you!

'That's it, Susan? I don't even know what it means!' I'll tell you what it means. Within every one of us lives a place of light and love that I have been calling the Higher Self. Hurtful life experiences have perhaps built walls to make it invisible. Nevertheless, the place of light and love is always there. Projecting the thought 'I greet the light in you!' allows you to get past the 'beautiful' or 'ugly' judgment of the other person and to connect with the beauty inside. Even if he or she seems obnoxious or unfriendly, 'I greet the light in you' is the phrase that opens our hearts and allows us to see beyond the darkness.

And there are other benefits. If you see the light in other people instead of the dark, you will automatically experience more light in your own life. It makes sense, doesn't it? So from this moment on, no matter how silly it may seem, practise **silently** projecting the thought 'I greet the light in you!' whenever you come into contact with other people. Whether you are driving your car, walking down the street or sitting in a restaurant, take a moment to look around and silently say to each person on whom your eyes happen to glance,

> *No matter what I see on the outside,*
> *I greet the light in you!*

It doesn't matter if this person is a drop-out asking for money or someone of obvious stature and wealth; it doesn't matter if this person is charming or rude; it doesn't matter if he conforms to our society's definition of attractive or unattractive; it doesn't matter if she is black, white, red or yellow, or what country he calls home. As we silently greet the light in others, we are projecting our own light into their world . . . and in so doing we are helping to heal not only their pain but ours as well.

A great time to do this exercise is when your patience is being really tried, such as when the assistant at the checkout is taking half an hour to ring up your shopping, or when the old man in front of you is driving at five miles an hour, or, on a more serious note, when you see someone who is being belligerent or unkind. At the beginning, sending loving thoughts seems frustratingly difficult, but just keep repeating to yourself,

> *No matter what I see on the outside,*
> *I greet the light in you!*

What you are really saying is: 'I'm focusing **only** on the part of you that is wonderful.' Aside from bringing our warmth and caring into the world, this kind of thinking:

1) lowers our blood pressure considerably;
2) allows us to feel compassion for all beings, including ourselves;
3) brings us into harmony with the flow of human experience instead of creating a block that reduces inner peace;
4) puts healing energy into the planet.

Not bad for one little phrase, 'I greet the light in you!'

To enhance this process, you might want to imagine yourself actually projecting from your entire body a healing warm light that envelops everyone you see. You can also project the image of healing warm light into any 'crowded room'. This act will instantly make the room a much friendlier place. I love using the warmth of an imaginary glow to break the ice around people's hearts, including my own.[1]

Another variation of 'I greet the light in you' is simply to walk down the street, silently saying 'I love you' to everyone you see. For those of you who object to the use of 'I love you' except when referring to specific other individuals, remember that we can love at many levels. In this case I am referring to a love of humanity that includes every human being on the planet – yes, even those whom you would like to punch in the face! A friend of mine practised this for one month and reported a dramatic shift in the way she felt about herself and her relationship to everyone around her. If you live in what is reputed to be an unfriendly city, you will be surprised to see how friendly it seems to become as a result of this exercise. The streets are at their most hostile when we build a wall around our hearts.

There are still other variations. One of my students imagines a heart pinned on everyone's clothes to remind her of the love they carry within them. Metaphysician Stewart Wilde tells us that, in order to deal with the negativity around him, he trained his mind to say the word 'peace' whenever he was in the presence of strangers. At the beginning he often forgot and had to remind himself over and over again, but in time this Everybody Training practice became part of his consciousness so that the word 'peace' came through automatically. He states, 'By wishing a million people "peace" then a million more, you create that energy within you, and gradually what you create is a peaceful world around you. The affirmation becomes real by its constant repetition and by the fact that you really mean it.'[2]

These heart-motivated 'gimmicks' are reassuring in this world of seeming alienation. They serve to wake us up to the fact that we are all part of the human family. The ultimate goal is to reach the point where we can no longer look at another person without, at some level, resonating the words 'I love you', 'I greet the light in you', or 'Peace'.

After you have mastered the art of telepathically greeting the light in other people and so begin feeling less alienated in the world out there, it's time to up the ante a bit. Now, as you walk down the street greeting the light in others, begin looking briefly into their eyes. You might even want to nod a sign of 'hello'. I have found in my many years of walking around the streets of New York, Los Angeles or wherever that seeing everyone as a 'person just like me', makes me feel really comfortable and alive. I smile, nod and make eye contact with old people, bag ladies, men and women off to work, policemen on the beat and so on.

I know danger sometimes stalks city streets – therefore I don't advise doing this on a dark street, late at night or when there is no one around. Yet, although it is very necessary to use common sense, I believe that when we use our 'safeguards' of confidence and love the streets are less dangerous than when we emit an energy of fear or suspicion. Any policeman will confirm that when you have a feeling of strength and belonging, the likelihood of being harmed is greatly diminished. Very often it is when we project our feelings of weakness, fear and separation that we draw trouble into our lives.

There are also many occasions during the day when you are engaged in face-to-face contact with other people. Begin looking them in the eye as you speak to them. Start with those that seem the least threatening, such as a bank clerk, waiter or waitress, or checkout girl in the supermarket. I don't mean that you should stare at people, nor does eye contact have to be constant. In fact, during conversation our gaze has a natural tendency to wander as we process different information in our mind. But this shouldn't prevent eye contact aimed at perceiving a common humanity: 'This is a person just like me.'

Remember to smile as you look someone in the

eyes, as it will take away the sense that you are staring. Don't be afraid that they will resent it – most people will welcome your warmth. Dale Carnegie reminds us why dogs are so popular: They go crazy with excitement every time they see you![3] You don't have to go crazy with excitement, but the point is well taken. Take a chance. Start smiling at people throughout the day. Let people know by your demeanour that they're part of the wonderful pot of energy that defines your world.

As you practise this exercise, always remember to replace any negative mental chatter with the positive thought projections. They are a *critical* part of the process. As you pass someone on the street or look them in the eye, feel the wonder in the fact that:

> *This is a person just like me, a human being with feelings, who has been rejected at times. This is a person just like me. He (or she) hurts, he feels, he has had many painful experiences, he wants to be liked, he needs approval.*

This kind of thought projection will create a far different effect from:

> *I hope he (or she) doesn't think I'm flirting. I wonder if he thinks I'm a jerk. I wonder why he didn't smile back. I must be really looking like a slob. Maybe I was staring too much, or maybe I wasn't smiling enough.*

In this scenario you focused only on yourself, never on the other person. Instead of moving you to the place of connection, this keeps you in the land of comparison, judgment and separateness. Speaking of which, the following inner thoughts don't work either:

> *He's (or she's) really sweet, but such a bad dresser!*
> *Maybe he's a little too short for me. Perhaps I*
> *should have gone to the guy standing over there.*
> *He seems to have it a little more together.*

The kind of energy that this creates is hardly a basis for meaningful connection.

Getting back to the 'crowded room' scenario, one question frequently asked in my classes is: 'What if you approach a person and he or she turns away from you?' My answer is never to take it personally. Immediately say *stop* to your Chatterbox, which may try to take away your confidence. The truth is that some people may be too nervous to respond in a friendly way. They may only know how to disconnect. Simply respect their feelings. Turn away, sending them compassion and love. Then try again with the next person.

Another common question is: 'What if some people mistake my gesture of friendship as a sexual approach?' Some people may indeed misunderstand. If so, simply apologize for the mix-up and explain what's true for you – that friendship was your only aim. (I'll talk more about these two questions in Chapter 6.)

I've also often been asked how we should carry ourselves when facing another person or group of people. My Everybody Training answer to that is simple:

> *Walk, sit and stand tall, delighted that you are*
> *who you are!*

There's nothing more you need to know. If you're not feeling particularly pleased with who you are, then simply act as if you were. Say to yourself,

> *'If I were really happy about who I am, how would I carry myself?'*

And then proceed to straighten those shoulders, take a deep breath and say to yourself at least ten times:

> *'I am a pleasure to know.'*

In this case, let your feelings follow your actions instead of the other way around. It works either way!

And now a few words about hugs – good, old-fashioned body warmth. There's a popular adage on the American workshop circuit: 'Four hugs a day for survival, eight hugs for maintenance, and twelve hugs for growth.' I am a great believer in hugs. I hug as many people as I can during the course of a day. I end business meetings by hugging everyone. At parties I hug people whom I have met for the first time. I hug my students. I hug my teachers. My husband and I hug constantly. The barriers that a hug brings down are enormous!

Self-esteem expert Jack Canfield tells the story of a man who conducted an experiment to see how many hugs he could give away on the streets of New York.[4] He was startled to find that everyone he asked for a hug gave him one, except one old lady who ran down the street in terror. Bus drivers gave him hugs, policemen gave him hugs, and so on. I guess people are more starved for hugs than we think they are – particularly bus drivers and policemen! I don't suggest that *you* conduct this experiment on the streets of a big city, but do take every opportunity you can to hug those around you.

If you feel happy about hugging, you probably don't have to pay attention to your hugging 'form'. You probably melt into the hug and are not concerned about what part of your anatomy is touching theirs. If you're not happy about hugging your body is probably very rigid, and so you are not deriving any nourishment from the body contact. Focus on relaxing your body. Start from the top of your head down to your toes and let yourself go. The image of melting into the hug is a good one: literally and figuratively defrost and let yourself warm into the other person's being. Again, focus on the thought projection:

> *I give you warmth and comfort as I take in the warmth and comfort you give to me. We are two hearts connecting as one.*

This is one exercise that you'll definitely come to love with practice.

Now that you have had some help with the 'mechanics' of connection, you are ready to stand eyeball to eyeball in front of another person and project your warmth and caring. The question is now: 'What do I say?'

Focus on being interested instead of interesting!

This means ask questions instead of trying to impress someone with how wonderful you are. You have probably already noticed that people who go on about themselves can be rather boring. The greatest acknowledgement you can give someone is to be interested in who they are.

Have you ever watched how some people converse at a party? Instead of focusing on the person with whom they're talking, they're busy looking around to see who else is at the party and to whom they should be talking or would rather be talking! They go through the motion of connecting, but they end up connecting with no one because they're so hung up on making impressions. Impression-making is truly the sad arena of 'empty suits'.

So, after you identify yourself, start your conversation with a question and pay attention when he or she answers.

- 'I'm a sales rep for Red Earth Industries. That's what brings me here. What about you?'
- 'I'm a friend of Joe's. How do you know the bride and groom?'
- 'I'm your neighbour from the flat opposite. How long have you lived here?'

So that you won't be considered an inquisitor, offer some information about yourself as the other person responds to your question. Even good talk show interviewers reveal a lot about themselves as they bring forth information from their guest. Very easily, a dialogue will be started. Not to worry.

Instead of the customary question, 'What do you do?', you might want to start with, 'What do you like doing?' This will elicit a picture of the inside of the person rather than their outer role. It is also a question that will bring forth a more lively kind of energy. Something you enjoy doing is something you can really get excited about. Talking about positive, meaningful things in each other's lives helps to pave the way for a desire to spend more time in each other's company.

Another approach is to offer a compliment. These usually work wonders, whether you are at a social or business situation. But make it genuine. Don't tell anyone that you love their intellect when the conversation hasn't gone further than the weather. Remember that we are not talking about a bag of tricks, but, rather, heart-felt tools of caring.

You can practise by giving at least ten compliments a day. Really get into it, and start complimenting people all over the place – we rarely do that. At home, in the office, or wherever, keep reminding people of how wonderful they are. When I gave this assignment in one of my classes, the feedback was heartening. My students' only lament was that they hadn't learned it earlier in their lives. They couldn't believe how good complimenting others could make them feel about themselves. So begin immediately with those ten compliments a day. There is *always* something about another person that you can genuinely admire. See how much good feeling you can put out there. Don't withhold any of it. People are fed by your positive vibes, and you'll be fed by the good feelings that are returned. Remember that the purpose of the compliment is not to make them like you, but rather to enrich their life in some way.

What we have been talking about throughout this chapter is the **the language of love** – Higher Self language that most of us are not accustomed to using. Some of it may seem very corny to those of us who have become cynical and sarcastic because of past hurts.

Many of us may even be embarrassed by the language of the Higher Self. Notice where your resistance lies; it is only through awareness that change is possible.

Whether or not you are at ease with the language of love, the lessons to be learned here are not automatic. We have been conditioned over a lifetime to speak **the language of fear**. Expertise in the language of love requires practice. I suggest that you first memorize the thought projections, then practise silently projecting them for ten minutes a day in the presence of others. As you continue to do this, they will eventually become automatic. Then, move forward with the rest of the exercise.

Remember, *never* be upset with yourself when it doesn't go as planned. Like all of us, you are a 'lover-in-training', and becoming a lover in the true sense of the word is a lifelong process. And, please, **keep a sense of humour about it all**. While these concepts are inherently very important to our wellbeing, we can all have a great deal of fun learning them if we remember to laugh constantly at our own folly – and that of the entire human race!

Just remember this:

People are aching to feel love from us.

This applies even to the passer-by in the street. It makes us feel so good to open our heart to others . . . to chat with people any time and almost anywhere . . . to send loving energy as we pass people in the street . . . to remark to someone in a department store that the outfit they're trying on looks great . . . to thank the street cleaner for keeping our city beautiful . . . to thank the waitress for her great service.

Sometimes people will respond hostilely. Make a game out of turning their hostility into love. It takes a lot of determination to keep your heart open and to act in a friendly manner when someone is responding hostilely. The chances are that your warmth will melt their heart. If not, simply understand that he (or she) doesn't know any other way to be in this world. What is important is that you do.

I was struck with these words of Ralph Waldo Trine, which were written in 1899: 'The word heaven means harmony. The word hell is from the old English "hell", meaning to build a wall around, to separate.'[6] While the meanings may differ today, it seems to me that, as we build walls around our heart, we indeed create our own hell. We separate ourselves off from all that is truly beautiful in this world. And what is truly beautiful is the love that we freely give and receive.

Remember that when we become proficient at the Higher Self form of connection, we become a magnet to other loving hearts. If we stay stuck in the Lower Self form of connection, we become a magnet to closed hearts – which is no fun at all! As you allow the reflection of your Higher Self to permeate your eyes, your smile, your hugs, your thoughts and your words, the results will be magical.

6

Some Enchanted Evening

There are many roadblocks to creating a successful relationship, and while we may blame circumstances 'out there' for our inability to connect with someone romantically, we would do better to look at some of the beliefs we hold inside. (Don't skip this chapter if you are already in a successful relationship – most of the concepts described here can be applied to other areas of your life too.)

From the time we were little boys and girls, our Somebody Training has fed us so many shoulds and shouldn't about each other. And as you already have discovered, old habits of thinking and behaving are hard to break. Therefore you may find yourself resisting some of the ideas I will be presenting here. As with anything, take in what works for you and let the rest go. Most importantly, keep an open mind, choosing, wherever possible, on the side of 'There are no strangers!'

IT ISN'T ABOUT LOOKS!

One of the myths our Somebody Training has taught us is that, if we aren't a perfect '10', love will be hard to find. We are convinced that if we don't meet the right requirements in terms of weight, hair colour, teeth, hips, penis length, bust size and so on, no one will love us – or we will eventually lose the love we already have! Why are we so quick to give credibility to the advertisements that are creating these ridiculous assumptions?

> All we need to do is to look around and see
> that finding love has nothing to do with looks!

As an experiment, the next time you walk down the street or go to a party, pay attention to the amazing array of couple-combinations that are right before your eyes as follows:

Couples in love
Attractive men with unattractive women.
Attractive women with unattractive men.
Older men with younger women.
Older women with younger men.
Older women with older men.
Short men with tall women.
Short women with tall men.
Short men with short women.
Fat women with thin men.
Fat men with thin women.
Women with cellulite with men with firm bodies.
Women without cellulite with men who have flabby bodies.

Women with gorgeous skin with men whose skin is
   acned.
Men with gorgeous skin with women whose skin is
   acned.
Balding men with gorgeous women.
Grey-haired men with grey-haired women.
Wrinkled women with gorgeous men.
Wrinkled men with gorgeous women.
Big-busted women with unsexy men.
Small-busted women with sexy men.

And the list goes on!

I'm being silly, but no sillier than most of us are in
judging our 'lovability' by our appearance. We agonize
over society's definition of physical 'flaws' that have
nothing to do with finding people to love. Once again
we see how our Somebody Training has conditioned
us to see people – including ourselves – primarily in
terms of the externals.

> When are we ever going to get it into our
> heads that looks play a very small part in our
> ability to create a loving relationship with
> members of the opposite sex?

As one young man said to me, 'Initially looks play a
part because that's all I've got to go on. But the minute
she opens her mouth, it's a whole new ball game.' Yes,
initially we may be drawn to someone because of their
looks. But within minutes, or even seconds, other
factors enter into the picture. I was once sitting in a
cab in New York waiting for the lights to turn green.
I looked out of the window and saw an incredibly

handsome man walking down the street. As I sat there with lustful thoughts roaming through my head, he started ridiculing an old woman who was walking towards him. In one instant, the most incredible transformation took place: this very handsome man turned ugly right before my eyes!

There is a wonderful line in Antoine de Saint-Exupery's story *The Little Prince*. 'What is essential is invisible to the eye.'[1] When it comes to love, truer words were never written. I look at my wonderful husband and I see only beauty in him . . . despite the physical flaws he sees in himself. My husband looks at me and sees only beauty . . . despite the physical flaws that I see in myself. Amazing when you consider that I have had a mastectomy! Can we be loved if we have only one breast? You bet we can! The other day I was pointing out to my husband a particularly beautiful woman walking down the street. He looked at her for a moment and said, 'I don't really find her attractive. She has one too many breasts!' With that he gave me a big kiss. (No, women out there it's not about breasts!)

Please hear what I am saying. We must stop worrying about the size of our breasts or penises and start paying attention to the size of our hearts! I know our conditioning is pretty hard to resist, especially with the artificial standards of 'beauty' on covers everywhere. But with awareness we can begin to turn our attention inwards, where it counts, instead of outwards, where it really doesn't.

To emphasize this point further: how many times have we asked ourselves as we watched a couple walking down the street, 'What does he see in her?' or 'What does she see in him?' Now you know! What they see in each other are those elusive invisible qualities that are essential to a love that works. And what are some of these qualities obviously worth cultivating? Here are a few to begin with:

self-esteem	warmth	kindness
aliveness	participation	caring
positiveness	consideration	courage
responsibility	sexuality	confidence
enthusiasm	authenticity	vulnerability
passion	vibrancy	humour
generosity	strength	lightness
love	compassion	empathy

Did you notice that I haven't said anything about underarm deodorant or make-up or clothes or weight or nail polish or perfume or aftershave or breasts or penises or skin or whatever other externals we focus too much attention on?

If you are still not convinced, the best I can do is leave you with a comforting thought I heard many years ago:

> We shouldn't worry about someone judging
> our bodies, because everyone else is too busy
> worrying about their own!

BE THE KIND OF PERSON YOU WOULD LIKE TO DATE!

Interesting notion, isn't it? What do I mean by that? Many negative men and women put in their order for a positive and emotionally healthy mate. Little do they know that their order is unlikely to be filled! Little do they know that negative energy draws negative energy (and positive energy draws positive energy). What you put out is what you attract. It's really that simple. Hence it stands to reason that:

> We should all make a list of those character-
> istics that we would like to see in a potential
> mate and then . . . go about cultivating them
> in ourselves.

It is important to pick up the mirror instead of the magnifying glass – not to judge ourselves, but to determine if we would fill our own requirements in a mate. Are we always complaining? Are we always looking for more, more, more? Are we jealous? Are we fun to be with? Are we out there enjoying all the beauty that life has to offer? Are we angry? Are we judgmental? Are we self-righteous? Do we have a chip on our shoulder? Are we trusting? Are we cultivating those qualities that are 'invisible to the eye?

Another crucial question to ask ourselves is: 'Are we needy?' Very often we *think* we are very loving people, when we are actually very needy. We 'give' purely for the purpose of buying love. We give, not from the openness of our heart, but because of the neediness caused by our own spiritual separation. And if you think people don't notice, you're absolutely wrong. They do notice, and they don't want the company of that kind of negative energy. As you have probably discovered for yourself, there is a something quality in a needy person that is very diffi-cult to be near.

If you recognize yourself as needy, what can you do

about it? The cure is obvious, but it takes time. It is one of those step-by-step processes that we focus on daily. It requires the creation of a rich life – one that has warm friends, meaningful activities, nourishing time alone, loving contributions to society, healing relationships with family and so on. In addition, a rich life requires commitment to all of the above, knowing that what we do in this life really makes a difference. It would help for you to learn how to create the framework of a rich life as I've outlined in *Feel the Fear and Do It Anyway*.[2] To keep neediness out of romance:

> It's important to have a life that is so full
> that the absence of romance doesn't destroy
> us.

This kind of life defines someone who cares about others, who is involved, who doesn't complain but appreciates the gift in all things, who listens and reaches out to help others, who respects him or herself, who feels passionate about certain projects, who appreciates just being alive. None of us would fill all of these requirements all of the time; we can learn, however, to fill many of these requirements much of the time.

When you lose your neediness, you become exciting to be with. You feel more powerful. When you walk into that crowded room, you attract emotionally healthy people into your life. And just as important,

> When you lose your neediness, you also take
> much of the risk out of love.

Rejection is always a possibility in love. But when your life is so full, the loss of a love will never destroy you. You may experience sadness, of course, and a temporary hole in your heart, but in a short time you'll reach out again, knowing that you have so much love to give to some other beautiful soul. You are, at last, in the blessed position of understanding that, no matter what happens relative to a relationship, **you can handle it!**

YOUR TYPE IS NOT YOUR TYPE

If you are not in a successful relationship, the likelihood is that your type is not right for you. You are probably turned on to people who are not compatible and turned off to people who think you are terrific and who would give you loving attention. It is my belief that despite *why* we are attracted to the wrong kind of person (and the reasons are varied), it is possible to see these attractions as unhealthy tastes that should be changed.

Let me use an analogy: I used to love my coffee with lots of sugar. That's the way coffee was 'attractive' to me. When I decided to give up sugar, I began drinking coffee without it. It tasted awful, but I persisted until finally I began to enjoy it that way. One day someone accidentally put sugar in my coffee and – you guessed it – it tasted awful! I had totally lost my taste for sugar in coffee. A silly analogy, perhaps, but changing my tastes in men happened in much the same way!

The best course of action, of course, is to stick with what we know is healthy for us and avoid that which is hurtful. To judge what's healthy, we should be asking ourselves questions such as:

- Is he or she a kind and loving person?
- Does he or she support the best of who I am?
- Do I feel strong and healthy when I am with him or her?
- Does he or she seem strong and healthy when with me?
- Am I constantly trying to change him or her?
- Is he or she constantly trying to change me?
- Do I feel comfortable being myself when I am with him or her?

We need to train ourselves to look at the Everybody Training qualities that have nothing to do with externals, but everything to do with heart and soul. This means that we should keep the company of loving partners until it really feels good. I've heard both men and women say after a first date, 'He (or she) was really very sweet, kind and loving . . . but I didn't hear any bells ringing.' You can imagine what I feel about those ringing bells – they're a warning to get your hearing checked! This is not to say that being sexually attracted to someone is not an important part of a relationship. It certainly is! But . . .

> It is far better to allow the sexual attraction to flow from the beauty of an evolving relationship than experience an instant attraction that quickly dissolves into disappointment and heartbreak.[3]

While I was not physically attracted to my husband when I first met him, the more the heart and soul within him was revealed to me, the sexier he seemed until he became – and remains – the most irresistible man around. So the next time someone approaches you at a party, try looking beyond the externals that have usually attracted you to people in the past. You might be surprised that the perfect partner for you is nothing like you ever imagined him or her to be. With that thought in mind, it's a good idea not to rule anyone out until you get beyond the nervousness of the first few dates (unless they are abusive in any way, of course). For better or worse, you might see a very different person emerge from the one who was there on that initial meeting.

A word about age: while a common complaint of women is that men like their women younger, it has been my experience that many men like their women older! Generally speaking, it's not the men who have the problem with older women, it's the women who have the problem with younger men. Why? They feel silly, more conscious of their wrinkles, threatened by younger women and so on. But as younger men with older women become more of an accepted fact, it is to be hoped that this self-consciousness will disappear.

When it comes to romantic relationships, I don't believe we should make an issue of age one way or the other. People have found love even where extreme differences of age have existed. Who are we to judge how people should or shouldn't find love? Yes, it's true that there are those who choose much older or younger mates for unhealthy reasons, such as to bolster a faltering ego. There is nothing for us to judge about that either. Such individuals have taken Somebody Training on board more than others, and therefore require external props to prove they are making the grade. If we can see the wounded child beneath the act, we would have more compassion. But I know from personal experience that it's sometimes hard.

I can't resist telling you of an experience I once had with such a man. I met him at a singles party and up came the subject of age. He told me he was forty-eight and I told him I was forty-one. He disdainfully responded with, 'I'd never date a woman over forty.' I looked him straight in the eye and lied, 'Oh, I know just what you mean. I wouldn't date anyone over forty either!' A look of anguish crept over his face as I excused myself and went merrily on my way. As you can imagine, my Higher Self wasn't too pleased – but I must admit, my Lower Self was absolutely delighted!

IT'S PERFECTLY OK FOR WOMEN TO MAKE THE FIRST APPROACH!

I can hear the resistance already, and certainly not from the men! Women, I ask you: Where is it written that men are supposed to be the prime pursuers in the dating and mating game? '*But*', you are saying,

> 'I've already tried that, and it didn't work.'
> 'Men get turned off if women approach them.'
> 'Men don't think it's feminine when we're so assertive.'
> 'My mother told me never to chase a man.'

I understand. When I was younger, I, too, believed that men should do all the approaching. But don't you think that, in today's world, this kind of thinking is glaringly out of place? Here we are, many years after the advent of the women's movement, still choosing to play manipulative games to try and get some man to select us instead of simply walking right up and making the selection ourselves.

I am amazed at the resistance so many women have to the idea of approaching men. They insist that men are really turned off by 'forward' women. I put it to the test and asked hundreds of men what they thought about it. And with few exceptions, I learned that:

Men love to have women approach them!

In fact, men desperately want women to help them out. They presented some very poignant statements about how it felt constantly having to make the initial approach:

'Sometimes I feel my heart is breaking.'

'Some women have treated me very badly when I approached them . . . and it hurts.'

'I get so nervous that, most of the time when I'm interested in someone, I get paralyzed and can't do anything about it.'

'It's so painful that sometimes I just don't bother.'

'It's hard. It is something you want to do and yet you are afraid of being rejected.'

'It's like the responsibility is all yours – and it really shouldn't be that way.'

'I think it should be a mutual thing. A lot of the time I just end up not doing it. I mean, why should I?'

> 'I think that I am more at ease with it now than
> when I was at college. But then it was so painful.'

Women have to understand that, however successful,
handsome, powerful, adorable, charming and attractive a man is or is not, the likelihood is that he is just
as insecure about approaching a member of the opposite sex as they are. (Once again, we learn, there are
no strangers!) The only difference is that our society
has, up until recently, demanded that *he* be the one
to do it. I suggest, therefore, in the interests of
humanity – and equality – women get in there and
help the men out.

> It is cruel and inhuman to allow men to be
> the only ones to put themselves out there to
> risk rejection. It is also cruel and inhuman
> for women not to be able to go after what
> they want!

Some women feel it is acceptable to approach a man
at a party, but that making the first phone call is a big
no-no. How did the men feel about that?

> 'I think it's great – it's a compliment.'
> 'No problem.'
> 'I enjoy it.'
> 'If a lady doesn't call me, I lose interest. I want to
> know she's interested enough to call.'
> 'I don't like always being on the offensive. I really
> appreciate it when a women helps out.'
> 'Theoretically, I think it would be great. It's never
> happened. I'm waiting.'
> 'It happens too rarely.'

One man reported that he met a woman at a party and they exchanged phone numbers, but he wasn't particularly interested and probably wouldn't have called her. The next day she called, and his estimation of her went up 100 per cent. He figured she had a lot going for her to have made the first move. They dated for quite a long time.

One woman told me that she had tried to approach men *twice* and been rejected on both occasions. This was enough proof to her that men don't like to be approached. I pointed out that it's lucky thing that *men* don't stop after two rejections, or there would be very little dating going on! Some men reported having been rejected by at least *ten* women before one accepted. Psychologist Dr David Burns tells us he was constantly rejected – in fact, he calls himself one of the most rejected men in northern California![4] One man suggested that women never have to worry about what to say when they approach a man: 'Just say anything. He'll be so relieved that he didn't have to make the approach!'

It is clear to me that it is something brewing beneath the surface that makes women so hesitant about approaching men – and the hesitation has little to do with the stated reason that 'men don't like it'. Let me suggest that what lies underneath the issue is that **women are frightened of putting themselves in the position of being rejected!** (It is so easy to blame others when we are consciously or unconsciously run by our fears.) Once women realize that it is their fear, not male attitudes, that stops them from approaching men, they at least know what they have to work on – and it isn't the men! Their next task is to learn how to 'feel the fear and do it anyway!'

You may be asking why, if making the first approach is so painful, women would want to change the conventions of dating. Why not let the men continue to bear the burden of making the initial approach? One good reason is that it removes the need of having to manipulate in order to get what we want. As women we can let go of all our 'drop the handkerchief' tricks and begin acting like authentic and more powerful selves. And, even more importantly, perhaps we'll get what we want – connection!

Before moving on, I don't want to leave you with the idea that *all* men will like the 'new woman' approach. Some are still locked in a double-standard mentality. But isn't this an important discovery to be made as quickly as possible? If I approached a man and he put me down for my 'forwardness', I would be totally put off by his 'backwardness' and quickly try the next person. When anyone puts us down for lovingly asserting who we are, it is our signal to transfer to someone else who will love the strength and openness and warmth of who we have become.

There's a very comforting message here for men: **if a woman doesn't approach you, it doesn't necessarily mean that she isn't interested.** It may simply mean that she is too nervous to make the approach. Don't take it personally. As you can see, many women have not yet reached the stage where they feel happy to break with tradition and approach men.

IT NEEDN'T BE A BIG DRAMA IF YOUR APPROACH IS TAKEN THE WRONG WAY

As I mentioned earlier, so many women and men express major concern over the possibility that someone they approach will assume they're interested only in sex. 'What if he thinks I'm easy?' 'What if she takes it the wrong way?' In most cases, we have little to worry about. If we are warm and interested, rather than 'sexual', our approach will rarely be taken the wrong way. But if it is . . . *so what*? As adults, what do we normally do when anyone takes anything the wrong way? We simply put them straight by explaining how we feel. And we do this in a caring manner:

> 'I'm sorry you took this the wrong way. I'm not interested in sex at this stage of the game. I'd really like to see if we can first be friends.'

> or

> 'I'm pleased you find me attractive, but I don't feel right getting sexually involved with someone I hardly know. Why don't we try being friends and see what happens from there?'

If this is agreeable to the person in front of you, great! If not, great! Once again, you will have discovered very early on whether or not this is someone you'd like to spend time with. No harm done. It's really that simple. So why the child-like concern?

I might point out that if your intention *is* sexual,

this doesn't make you a bad person. **Nor is someone else a bad person if their primary interest in you is sexual**. That is simply the stage they have arrived at in their own personal process of evolving. Why do we assume that someone is putting us down if their interest in us is only physical? In a sense it is a denial of a very beautiful part of our being, our delicious sexuality. (I am not, of course, talking about instances of physical or verbal abuse.)

When I was younger, I was emphatic about the fact that I wanted men to be interested in my mind, not my body. But it certainly doesn't upset me now if someone is interested in my body as well – you see how age matures one! I have no intention of acting on their show of interest, as my marriage is precious to me, but their interest is always reassuring. I'm probably one of the few feminists who warms to those wolf whistles from building sites. The workmen always get a big smile and a wave from me in return.

One of the reasons that so many women object to sexual advances is that they feel they are being used as a sexual object. I have sad news: as students of Somebody Training, we all have been taught to 'use' each other for one reason or another. Men have indeed used women as sex objects – and women have indeed used men as success objects. In these changing times, the opposite now applies as well. As we take more responsibility for following the rules of Everybody Training, ultimately our need to use each other as objects will diminish considerably.

By the way, some men report that they come on to women sexually because they believe women expect it; and for some women, this is true. For example, I have often heard women complain after several dates if the man hadn't yet made a sexual advance. What was wrong with him? Was he gay? Did he have another girlfriend? Didn't he find her attractive? They hadn't considered the fact that he could have been shy, or considerate, or more interested in developing a friendship before jumping into a sexual relationship. It is also true that more and more men are complaining of being used as sexual objects.

The frightening reality of the AIDS epidemic is relevant, too. Before this universal crisis, whether to have sex early in a relationship was purely an emotionally based decision. Now it is a health issue as well. Great care has to be taken in choosing someone to go to bed with, as well as in deciding what to do when we get there. As with all crises, we need to look at the thread of something positive that the situation offers. In terms of AIDS, many of us have discovered a more comfortable new kind of 'getting to know you' ritual. We have learned to put more emphasis on friendship than on sex, which has proved to be a very positive thing.

DON'T TRUST BODY LANGUAGE

Many books have been written about how to read body language, particularly in the area of romance. But knowing what I know about boy meets girl, I question how body language can be read. For example, many women report that they turn away from the men they are most interested in knowing simply because they feel so insecure. Now, in terms of body language, one would assume that if someone turns away from you they are not interested. Sometimes that is true, but sometimes it obviously is not.

One woman in a singles group reported that she is able to be warm and welcoming with every man in the group *except* the one who truly interests her. Every time he looks her way she averts her eyes and turns away, her heart pounding madly. I'm sure the poor man is convinced that he is the only one in the group in whom she has no interest whatsover! Similarly, one man reported that he can be a wonderful flirt except with someone he really likes. In that situation he immediately turns away; and all too often, by the time he regains his composure and turns back again, she's gone. As you can see, it's hard to trust body language when the person who most wants to meet you is the one who is the quickest to turn away from you!

So what's the solution? It's easy, yet sometimes hard to see.

> Go after what *you* want, despite what someone's body language is telling you. Of course, the risk of rejection is there (and you'll handle that!); on the other hand, you may be pleasantly surprised to find someone to love.

STOP TRYING TO BE A MIND READER

'What do women want?' 'What do men want?' These frequent questions always get an unexpected answer from me:

> It doesn't matter what they want. Be yourself and see who shows up!

Trying to act the way we think others want us to act is a futile activity. The reason is that everyone has different 'wants' in terms of a partner. For example, some men want passive women, while others prefer assertive women. Some women want intellectual men, others more physical men. Some people want to be approached assertively; others prefer softer tactics. So what's a person to do? Given that everyone has different tastes, it makes sense to **be yourself at all times rather than trying to second-guess the other person!**

Simple, isn't it? Yet I watch men and women trying so hard to figure out what the other sex wants and then twisting themselves all out of shape to fit the imagined requirements. And what's the only possible result? **We ultimately learn to dislike ourselves (and the other person as well) for not loving and honouring who we truly are.**

Janet, an assertive salesperson, initially acted very passively to the men she dated because she thought that was what they liked. When her assertive nature eventually burst forth after having been cooped up for so long, the men didn't like what they saw. This further reinforced her belief that men like passive women. She hadn't understood the obvious: if she acted in a passive way, she would draw a man who likes passive women. If she honoured her true assertive self and put it out in the world for all to see, she would attract a man who liked her assertive self!

Janet figured it out when she was spending time with Kevin, a man in whom she had no real romantic interest. Because she wasn't that attracted to him she dropped many of her acts, not really caring whether he liked who she was or not. Much to her surprise, the more 'real' Janet became, the more Kevin was attracted to her. In a short time, Janet discovered what a joy it was to be herself – with all her human strengths and frailties – and have somebody love all of it! One year later, Janet and Kevin were married.

I can guarantee you that if you honour the essence of who you really are and proudly let it shine through, your chances for a successful 'match' are greatly increased. In the end,

> It's not only about who *you* are attracted to. *Equally important is that they be attracted to the truth of who you are!* Only in this way can the circle of love be complete.

With all of the above in mind, here's something to remember when putting our true selves out there in the name of love . . .

REJECTION SHOULDN'T BE TAKEN PERSONALLY

As I stated earlier, every time we approach someone new, whether for business, friendship or romance, we risk rejection, but it seems to hurt most in the area of romance. So, when we approach a potential partner, we have to go into high gear with the important affirmation:

> *No matter how this person reacts to me, I know I am a worthwhile person.*

If you are rejected, they may be involved with someone else, or prefer redheads, or they could be too nervous to respond to your approach, or whatever. **Their reason is irrelevant. Your reaction is what's important.** Remember that we cannot control the way anyone acts towards us; we can only control our reactions. Remember, too, that there are lots of other people out there. This is not a 'one drink of water in the desert' kind of world. If someone is not interested in getting to know us, there is always someone else who *is* looking for love.

Consider this

If you are *constantly* getting rejected by potential partners, think of it as an opportunity to look at the 'vibes' that *you* are sending out to other people. Are you sending messages of anger, sarcasm, insensitivity, 'walk over me' weakness, neediness, or anything else that would turn people off?

> All of us in one way or another wear our heart on our sleeve. And whether our heart is open or closed is revealed very easily to those around us.

If we are sending out positive vibes, as a general rule we get positive vibes in return. Of course, there are exceptions, but if you are *always* getting rejected, it is a signal that you still have some work to do on yourself. **What is important is that you see it as an opportunity for growth, not as a flaw for which to criticize yourself.**

DO WHAT YOU ENJOY DOING AND THE DATES WILL FOLLOW

Where is the best place to meet people? It's not at home waiting for Prince or Princess Charming to show up. You really need to put yourself out there where people who you would like are to be found.

> The best place to meet people is wherever people congregate to do the things you enjoy doing. And *not* in places where people congregate to do the things you don't enjoy doing.

For example, it is self-defeating to go on an Outward Bound course to meet someone if you hate the outdoors. You might find a mate, but you may also find yourself constantly convered with mosquito bites – all part of the package of a relationship set up in this way. I was once asked if a bar was a good place to meet people. My answer was, 'Definitely yes, if you love the bar scene and would spend time there anyway. Definitely no, if you hate the bar scene and wouldn't spend time there anyway!'

I am firmly of the belief that 'Opposites attract' is in general a misleading statement. With certain personality traits, this may be true. For example, Carol is an assertive woman while Steve is more laid back; this combination of opposites works beautifully. But where they are very similarly aligned is in their values and preferred lifestyle. These factors are the key to harmonious living. Carol and Steve enjoy doing the same activities together. So if you do what you like best, it is more likely that you will meet someone who will share your values and chosen lifestyle.

Also keep in mind that a formal setting isn't necessary. As you practise the techniques in Chapter 5, you'll be able to strike up a conversation in a supermarket, the waiting room at the dentist's, on the bus or wherever. Seize the opportunity to be friendly. When we are friendly, we meet the nicest people! (Of course, you must only attempt this in safe conditions.)

My suggestion is:

> Do *nothing* in your life simply for the purpose
> of meeting someone. Do something simply
> because you love doing it . . . because it
> expands the richness of your life . . . because
> it brings you pleasure.

When your primary purpose is to meet someone, your expectation is almost guaranteed to reduce your pleasure in the activity itself. And if Prince or Princess Charming is nowhere to be found, you will go home greatly disappointed. So do yourself a favour and take the pressure off by simply following your heart's desire. It is very likely that a person to love will appear when and where you very least expect it.

It is important to understand that the world is filled with people who are looking for love. Don't believe people who tell you that the likelihood of finding someone is next to zero. Look around at the enormous amount of marriages between people of all ages. It surely can't be as bad as all that!

Even if there were shortages of available men or women, the truth is that some people would always find someone great to date and others wouldn't. It has nothing to do with numbers. On a recent lecture tour, I appeared on a television show featuring three women who complained they could never find any decent men to date and three other women who always found great men to date. All six women were physically attractive and successful in their careers. The difference was clearly in those invisible qualities that either attract people or turn them off. I pointed out the different 'vibes' of the two groups of women. The three who had no problems finding great men to date were open, sunny, fun, positive and obviously really liked people, men included. The other three were sarcastic and judgmental, and were carrying a big chip on their shoulder. It is very clear to me that if the sign on your heart says 'welcome', the love will come pouring in.

DEVELOP KINDNESS TOWARD MEMBERS OF THE OPPOSITE SEX

I guarantee that, unless you truly think about and treat members of the opposite sex with kindness and respect, you're not going to develop a healthy romantic relationship with any of them. This seems elementary. But the very fact that we have something called 'the war between the sexes' is a not-so-subtle clue that for too many of us a healthy relationship is virtually impossible. One is seldom loving to the enemy.

Many men and women are truly angry with one another, some more openly than others. Each claims good cause for anger. Yes, women, it's true that some men will walk all over you. And, yes, men, it's true that some women will walk all over you as well. But, in the end,

> We can't blame anyone for walking all over
> us. We can only notice that we're not getting
> out of the way.[5]

It is amazing what happens when we stand tall, take charge of our lives and act with integrity toward ourselves and others. Our lives begin to work, and we begin to attract people with the same kind of positive energy. And, contrary to popular opinion, there are plenty of people with positive energy around. But to find them, it is essential that we pick up a mirror (instead of a magnifying glass) and work through our anger, lack of trust, judgment, self-righteousness and neediness, all of which are barriers to loving one another.

The more love we project to members of the opposite sex, the more loving people we will attract. The opposite is true as well. It is only when we finally learn to let go of our anger and open our hearts to each other that we can find wonderful people to love. That's just the way it is.

7

Friendship: The Safety Net of the Heart

'My marriage was over. The feeling of emptiness inside of me was hard to ignore. I desperately needed to talk to someone to help ease
the pain. I picked up the phone to reach
out . . . but I realized there was no one there.
And so I discovered at the age of thirty-two,
after ten years of marriage, that I didn't have
any friends, not really. While there were many
women I cared about and spent a lot of time
with, there had never been any authentic
sharing between us.'

As I listened to Betty's story, I thought back to my own
which was remarkably similar. My first marriage was a
time of great activity for me – doing post-graduate
research, raising two children, trying to make my
marriage work, entertaining my husband's business
contacts and working part-time. It wasn't as though
there weren't people in my life; there were too many!
Yet, because I hid so many of my feelings behind my

well-defended act, it was actually the loneliest time of my life.

I have since learned how to create a deep feeling of bonding with my friends. We have become a source of great love, support and empowerment to each other. As a result, I rarely feel a sense of loneliness. I have learned to embrace friendship in the gentle and soothing way that Sam Keen embraces it:

> 'Philia (friendship) seems at first to be the most modest of the modes of love. It is as quiet as a shared cup of tea or glass of beer . . . It is shared conversation. No howling on the full moon. No demonic explosions of contradictory passions. Friendships make gentlewomen and gentlemen open and fearless enough to give and receive as a matter of daily inter-course. It lacks romantic trappings, does not demand beautiful partners or youth. In fact, it is the solace of those who have nothing else. And when it is strong enough, we need little else – besides bread and butter.'[1]

A beautiful statement about friendship, to be sure. And in this world of constant change and rootlessness, we need the solace of friendship perhaps more than ever before. I have heard it said that friendship may even be more important than romantic love. I am thankful we don't have to make a choice between the two. Both clearly contribute something very special, very different, very important and very pleasurable to our lives.

There are different levels of friends. First, there are those connected to us only by shared activities. These are the people with whom we study, go to a football match, shop, raise our children, go hiking and so on, but who do not necessarily share the truth of who we are. Other friends are connected to us only by history. Some go all the way back to our youth, and we hold a special place in our heart for them. The tie of a common background may be there, but the authentic sharing often is not.

Friendships based on shared activities and historical ties are wonderful to have, but unless they are 'deepened', they are not enough. Our circle of friends must also include those with whom we can openly and authentically share, heart and soul, the truth of what is going on with us behind our acts. I'll call these **soul-friendships**. Naturally, if we can create soul-friendships with our activity mates and our way-back-when mates, this is wonderful. (A beautiful example of this is given at the end of the chapter.) If not, it is important to look elsewhere.

Soul-friendships are **Higher Self friendships**, not to be confused with Lower Self friendships which thrive mostly on shared complaints and commiseration. When people talk about having close friends, very often this is the type they are talking about. While they share their feelings, primarily their anger and hurt, their sharing is usually in the form of blame. Their conversations are characterized by a lot of 'Would you believe he (or she) did this to me?' type of questions and a lot of 'You poor thing!' type of responses. They become **'complaint mates'**, and in that there is a feeling of great closeness. The problem is that there is no healing when we go along with each other's victim act. Blaming others makes us powerless; hence complaint mates offer only a continuation of our misery. They offer few positive avenues for picking up our power, taking responsibility for our lives and moving forward with love. That's the bad news.

The good news is that, although filled with negativity, this type of friendship can be considered a step in the right direction. At least it's characterized by an **openness** about anger and pain that is often absent from relationships with activity mates and way-back-when mates. And if complaint mates can abandon their attitude of blame, they can often upgrade their friendship from the level of the Lower Self to the Higher Self, thus creating a soul-friendship that ultimately can help us to heal our lives.

Soul-friendships require us to make some major break throughs: those of us who are closed need to break through our fear of opening up and allow ourselves to become vulnerable to someone else; those of us who constantly complain need to stop blaming and begin taking responsibility for our experience of life. Not easy! But the benefits of soul-friendships are worth the effort and courage it takes to create them. For example,

1) Soul-friendships are the safety net of the heart

Despite what happens in our family, business or love relationships, good friends are always there – and the supply is unlimited. Having a number of soul-friendships guarantees a shoulder to cry on and a voice to remind us that we need never be alone.

2) Soul-friendships provide the wellspring from which all other relationships in our life can be nourished

With the help of a rich pool of soul-friendships we can work out our insecurities and fears and gather strength, integrity, clarity and love. We can then carry these healing attributes into all our relationships – with parents, partners, children, colleagues and even the 'strangers' with whom we come into contact every day of our lives.

3) Soul-friendships allow us to know ourselves better

In trying to tell our friends who we are and what we are feeling, we explain it to ourselves as well. Good friends also provide a valuable source of feedback; they don't allow us to get away with our act. They lovingly demand the truth about who we are. And most of the time, we take feedback from friends much better than from others, particularly our parents, partners or children.

4) Soul-friendships provide the school in which we learn to love ourselves (a prerequisite to loving others)

Friends are the mirror reflecting the truth of who we are. Through mutual sharing we truly learn that 'you are me and I am you'. And, by definition, as we cultivate love and compassion for our friends we cultivate it for ourselves as well.

This last 'benefit' brings up the importance of having a number of soul-friendships of the same sex. Same-sex friendships offer an opportunity that cannot be found with members of the opposite sex. That is, they provide a **self-identification** essential for allowing us to see the strength and beauty inherent in being male or female.

When we bond woman to woman, we reach deep into the essence of our true (rather than society-imposed) femininity; and when we bond man to man, we reach deep into the essence of our true masculinity. It is only then that we find a place that feels like **home** . . . a place of genuine belonging in the grand scheme of things.

- It is here that we touch the power with which our own gender is endowed.
- It is here that we stop feeling second-class as men or women.
- It is here that we gather self-esteem and begin to feel the awesome contribution we can make as human beings **because** of our sexual identification.
- It is here that we can get in touch with a deep, deep level of connectedness that, because of biological and cultural reasons, members of the opposite sex cannot provide for us.

If our friends belong primarily to the opposite sex, it suggests that we are not comfortable with the truth of who we are, gender-wise. So many men say they don't like men and prefer the company of women, and vice versa. This is ultimately a harsh put-down of the self.

> In order to love ourselves, it is essential that we love our gender as well. It's all part of the package!

Once we feel love for who we are, gender-wise, we can
then come together – man and woman – knowing that
we have something wonderful to offer each other. This
is far more nourishing than coming together humbly
praying that some of the beauty and strength of the
other person will somehow rub off on us – which, if
you haven't noticed, is one of the hidden agendas of
many men and women interacting. So we need that
time together – man to man and woman to woman –
to reflect to each other our inherent value as human
beings, so that we don't have to beg for it somewhere
else.

Psychotherapist Richard Prosapio talks of the value
of men interacting with men in order to relate better
to women:

> 'It's as if we each have to find ourselves –
> and we'll be right back. It has to do with
> standing in the sun for a moment and seeing
> your own shadow, not blended with someone
> else's but separate. And then moving out
> from that place, we (men and women) can
> come together.'[2]

And when we come together from that place of
'standing in the sun for a moment', we have much to
learn from each other. Men and women have been
conditioned very differently in our Somebody-Trained
society, and as a result see the world from very different
perspectives – a fact which, in our frustration and insecurity with each other, we often forget. For example,
women are trained to be more nurturing and men to
be more success-oriented. As we begin to share our
differing 'realities', each of our visions widens to take

in more and more of the whole. Our Somebody Training, with its emphasis on different roles, taught us to be half-people; soul-friendships between men and women can put us on the road to wholeness.

Also, as we share the truth of who we are we learn to respect one another and to feel compassion for the inner wounds that the 'shoulds' and 'shouldn'ts' of our Somebody Training have inflicted on men and women. The pain and insecurity aren't restricted to only one of the sexes, as some of us may believe. Along with this feeling of respect and compassion comes the end of the soul-destroying 'war between the sexes'.

Yes, soul-friendships create incredible richness in our lives. Too many of us, however, don't have a clue how to create or be in a friendship of this kind. Some women are ahead of men in this department. Because of the women's movement, they have gathered together in groups and have learned how to open up to one another. As a result, they have created wonderfully supportive and nourishing soul-friendships. Other women, however, are still enmeshed in the unhealthy 'complaint mate' syndrome that I spoke of earlier; that is, they use their friendship to support their complaining. Still others, like most men, are unable to share their deepest feelings with anyone. This means that all of us – men and women alike – have a lot more to learn about friendship.

With this in mind, it is important to keep reviewing the 'essentials of connection' discussed in Chapter 5. The following tips will also help hasten the joyful, yet sometimes frightening, task of forming new friendships and deepening old ones. First, it is helpful to remember that, aside from the issue of sex, making friends is very similar to dating.

- **Just as in dating**, there is an initial 'chemistry' between people which either attracts us or repels us.

- **Just as in dating**, if we're not picking friends who bring out and support the best in who we are, our 'chemistry' is wrong. 'Our type is not our type!'

- **Just as in dating**, our friends are a mirror to our emotional state. If the people we pick are supportive and loving, we're projecting positive self-worth. If the people we pick are negative and pull us down, we're projecting a lack of self-worth.

- **Just as in dating**, it is important to risk rejection and take responsibility for making the first approach. If he or she doesn't seem interested after a few calls, move on to the next person.

- **Just as in dating**, it is important to remember that, no matter how anyone acts towards you, you are a worthwhile person.

- **Just as in dating**, there is an initial infatuation period during which your new friend can do no wrong.

- **Just as in dating**, there comes the time when the 'honeymoon' is over and you start to see the flaws . . . at which point you either work through the disillusionment and become real friends, or you go your separate ways.

- **Just as in dating**, it is important to be who you are. If someone likes who you are, you have a new friend. If someone doesn't like who you are, no problem – just move on to the next person. Eventually you end up with a friend who wants to be with you **because of who you truly are**, not who you pretend to be or who they want you to be.

- **Just as in dating**, friends can hurt you. With healthy self-esteem, you pick yourself up and find some new friends.
- **Just as in dating**, the way you make conversation is by being interested instead of interesting.
- **Just as in dating**, friendships must be cared for and tended, not put on the back burner. They need an intentionality behind them. You need to shower them with love. Whether you write a letter, make a phone call, buy a gift or pay a compliment, it is essential to let your friends know that they are in your heart.
- **Just as in dating**, your contact has to be regular. It is important to connect not only in a crisis, but just for the purpose of saying 'Hello, I really care about you.'
- **Just as in dating**, it's important to keep working on your self-esteem so you don't become needy. Neediness is a turn-off, no matter what the situation.
- **Just as in dating**, you want to draw friends who build you up instead of diminish you, who help make you feel confident instead of frightened, and strong instead of weak, who don't habitually complain but who appreciate the beauty in their lives, who see life's setbacks as opportunities for growth instead of failure, and who can share their emotions.

Now that I've told you some of the similarities between creating friendships and dating, let me tell you an interesting difference. Now that I've told you some of the similarities between creating friendships and dating, let me tell you an interesting difference. While dating is familiar and readily accepted, friendships have taken a back seat in our busy lives. If we have friends, they often seem to be acquired through our everyday activities, few of us actually seek them out. Friendships have taken a back seat in our busy lives. If we have friends, they seem to be acquired through our everyday activities; few of us actually seek them out.

Potential friends may back away for other reasons as well. For example, along with commitment and intention, soul-friendships also imply responsibility. It's much easier to turn our backs and not care. So it's sometimes necessary to cultivate friendships slowly and with great sensitivity to another's resistance. Remember that becoming part of other people's lives takes time. At the moment their plate may be full, their schedule crowded. As you keep inviting them into your life, however, they may eventually join you in friendship. Or maybe not. Just remember that if someone does not want to include you in his or her circle of friends, the reasons may well not be personal.

For example, my life is extremely full. If I am to honour present commitments to myself, my loved ones, my work and my community, I have to be very careful not to overload myself with more people than I can give adequate attention and love. So if I refuse the hand of someone's friendship, it has nothing to do with them personally. It has only to do with my full life.

If you're the one resisting the time and commitment that soul-friendships require, it's very important to push through the resistance and make friendship one of your priorities. Friends need to spend blocks of time together – one-to-one – to nourish the relationship. Short blocks of time rarely allow intimacy to occur. Most of us need a warming-up period to allow us to 'get down' into real feelings. Initially, we talk about surface 'happenings' in our lives. 'Yesterday I did this' or 'I just changed my job', or 'My wife hasn't been feeling very well', or whatever. Only after the stories are out of the way do we get into the deeper levels of our feelings. And it is here that we find our soul-connections with one another.

I have found that one of the easiest ways to get friends to open up to you on a feeling level is for you to open up to them first (and the following chapter introduces you to a great way of learning how to open up). In so doing, you create a safe space for them to come out of their shell. If someone can't handle your openness very well, that's fine. Back off and enjoy them as an activity mate. More than likely, however, they will respond to your openness by revealing more of themselves.

The greatest benefit that can be derived from our friendships occurs when we help each other to be the best that we can be, as opposed to sharing each other's complaints and feelings of helplessness. So when friends constantly complain, gently guide them into taking more responsibility for their lives. If the complaints continue, it's time to find some other friends. (You will find that the more positive and loving you become in life, the less you will want to be with friends who are constantly being negative.) Don't feel guilty about leaving them behind – remember that they'll always find someone else to complain to.

I want to end this chapter with the voices of three young women who were able to transform their superficial, and sometimes hurtful, relationships into a nourishing soul-friendship. Grace, Rachel and Leslie are old college friends, now twenty-nine years old. Other than the common college experience, their backgrounds are very diverse – three different religions, three different family experiences (one's parents are divorced, one's parents are together but very unhappy, one's parents are happy together but very repressed), three different economic backgrounds, three different occupations. Each, however, is similarly endowed with a huge amount of attractiveness, enthusiasm, intelligence and heart.

After being 'on and off' friends for eleven years, they decided that they wanted their friendship to be more than it was. All three women had begun their own path toward wholeness by attending CoDA meetings (as discussed in Chapter 3). This was a great start in helping to upgrade the level of their friendship. To deepen it even further, they decided to make use of a workbook entitled *The 12 Steps: A Way Out*,[3] which is described as a working guide for people from addictive or dysfunctional families (and we now know that all Somebody-Trained families are dysfunctional!).

The three women committed to meet once a week for six months, each week having completed an agreed upon section of the workbook. Their time together was spent simply reading what they had written. The reading was not meant to trigger an open discussion. If something was triggered or left incomplete, or if they needed to get some perspective on something, they talked about it. But basically they were there to share their feelings through their writing.

It is clear to me that their commitment to transform their superficial and sometimes hurtful friendship into a soul-friendship has paid off enormously, as the following excerpts from my interview with them demonstrate. My first question was 'What did your friendships look like earlier?'

Grace: Earlier, I didn't have many female friends. What does that say about myself? That I didn't like myself very much then.

Rachel: I was frightened approaching women. I was afraid of being rejected . . . afraid of being vulnerable. My mother and I weren't very good friends. So I didn't know how to be good friends with another woman. My sisters and I weren't close, either. My friendships in school always turned out badly. I remember girlfriends always competing with me, putting on an act. One of them actually created imaginary letters from an imaginary boyfriend. Another one used to say terrible things behind my back . . . that I was drinking, having sex, doing drugs or whatever.

Grace: I just didn't value friendships with women a few years back. I never considered myself a good friend . . . because I really burned my girlfriends. When they were no longer useful, I would just disappear. I stopped returning their phone calls. I moved often, or found new friends. Perhaps it was fear of being vulnerable if I got too close. Also, I didn't choose appropriate people to have friendships with. Part of that was my way of rebelling against my parents. My friendships were also superficial because I never asked for or gave support . . . I didn't think I needed it. I was into being independent. I had to prove I was sufficient on my own. I was enough. A lot of women are seeking independence, and they refuse to ask for help . . . I think it's sad. The only person I needed was a man for things other than friendship. What I realize now is that I do need other women – and men – and their friendships. And it's OK to need that and I don't feel weak. I feel strong that I could ask for that.

Leslie: I also used to be superficial in my friendships because I thought if they really knew me, they wouldn't want to be around me. I thought I had to be funny, or buy them presents, or whatever. I didn't think they were there because I had something to offer. I think a lot of the genuineness in our friendships now comes from the growth of our self-esteem.

I asked them to expand on what makes friendships different now.

Grace: For the first time, there is an equality. In the past, I was either being helped or helping. There was always a weaker and a stronger. I find now my friendships are based on mutuality. Sometimes one is weak and sometimes one is strong, and we help each other.

Leslie: In the beginning I idolized Rachel, as though she was my big sister. I would go to her with a problem. I couldn't imagine her coming to me with a problem. I now realize my opinion really matters.

Grace: I can go to my friends now and ask for help. I think that's what's different. We've developed a trust so that when in need we can reach out and ask for emotional support. Whatever the problem is. I've reached a point where I really welcome that kind of support. It was always there, but I just didn't allow it into my life.

Leslie: I was a very flaky friend. I used to come up with all sorts of excuses to get out of commitments with friends. Now my word really means something.

Grace: My ability to form real friendships with women started, I think, with my acceptance that I am a woman. Because that really bothered me for a long time. I thought women had the short end of the stick, and I wasn't interested in being one. Or doing anything that was feminine. I was very masculine. Now I've learned to value my femininity – my womanhood. And that's made all the difference in the world. I think my initial attitude was a result of looking at the relationship my parents had. My mother was very subservient and he was the boss. I didn't want to be in her position, but that was the only model I had. Either/or. So I became 'Dad', tough and distant. I finally reached a point where I realize that it doesn't have to be either/or any more. I've got far enough away from my family and my home to realize that there are other options. I see different kinds of relationships and other kinds of women. There are dynamics out there that are certainly different from what took place in my home.

Leslie: The three of us have been actively stepping back and getting better perspectives on our families. I'm reaching the point where I am willing to be in the dark about what was really going on when I was young and am opening to the fact that maybe my perception is an illusion . . . or a misinterpretation of what really went on. It pays to look back and say, 'Whatever went on, I am no longer going to be a victim of it,' then heal the wounds and move on.

Grace: We are all in some way caught up with what we came from. But as adults we can choose not to react and to live a different sort of life. Friends can help each other to do that.

Leslie: If I know that something is really off with me and I am reacting inappropriately about something, I can turn to Rachel or Grace and they can pinpoint what it is. I just say, 'Something is going on here and I can't see it.' And they both know me well enough to know what pushes my buttons. A couple of weeks ago I called Grace and said, 'I was really upset with my boyfriend last night and I'm still angry and I don't know what is going on with me.' Grace was funny and she was great. She saw exactly what was going on. And we could laugh about it and lighten up about the whole situation. And my anger, which was really inappropriate, went away.

Grace: It gives me great comfort that they are in my life and that I can turn to them when I need to. We were friends before, but at a very superficial and at times dysfunctional level. None of us knew how to ask for help from one another. Even if we felt comfortable doing that, none of us were self-aware enough to know what we needed help for!

Leslie: It's got to the point that I can solve problems by just talking to Rachel and Grace in my head. There have been times when I have needed one of them and they weren't around. So I'd say to myself, 'If this was their problem and they called me, what would I say?' And the answer comes through, loud and clear. What happens is that I remove myself from the middle of the problem and become my own observer. This takes me immediately out of the heavy drama of the situation. And I can think much more clearly. I'm learning to trust my own inner wisdom.

(Lesile's comments here can be seen as another version of 'lonely me' and 'me watching lonely me' discussed in Chapter 4.)

Leslie: We have learned to tell the truth to each other. Sometimes in my writing I would notice myself saying, 'I don't want to write that!' And then I'd say to myself, 'Who am I hiding from? It's not as if they don't know this. It's not as if they haven't felt this.' And then I'd go on to expound in great detail on the very thing I was hesitant to write about. I'd think, why am I committing my time and their time and not telling the truth? I'd only be cheating myself. And the more I am willing to risk and the more I am willing to open up, the more I get out of it.

Rachel: When you tell the truth about something, it becomes less frightening. Whatever problem it was for you – your behaviour, your guilt, your shame – when you write it down and share it and hear from the other person, 'Oh, yes, I've done that before' or 'I've felt like that before', then you're able to let it go.

Leslie: When you tell your deepest, darkest secrets and people don't recoil in horror, like you think they would, you become healed. There is a personal inventory in the workbook, 'a searching and fearless moral inventory of ourselves', and I was really nervous doing it. The instructions are to share it with yourself, God and one other person. I finally did it with Grace and was really nervous about sharing my truth. What I discovered was that there wasn't anything in my personal inventory that Grace hadn't experienced herself. Beforehand, I had visions of her never calling me again, never seeing me again. It turned out that we had so much fun doing it together. And it made us feel even closer.

Grace: I've learned that everything I have ever done in my life, no matter how bad I thought it to be, was done to love me. Sometimes my ideas of loving myself were a bit distorted, but at the base of all my behaviour was the motivation to protect myself and find love the best way I knew how.

Leslie: I really cringe at some of my past behaviour and feel sad about the part of me that felt that was how I had to behave. Grace helped me to see I had no way of knowing that there was a different way to be. She helped me see that I did what I did because it's what I thought I had to do to get love. It's really helped me have more compassion for that scared, sad little girl inside who was so needy.

Rachel: What we are doing in this writing group is learning how to forgive ourselves and to love ourselves . . . through supporting each other and supporting our souls. It helps us to say, 'Oh yes, I was behaving abominably but I was doing the best I could.' And now I can love and forgive myself and act more appropriately. And we laugh about it, which takes a lot of weight from it. For the most part we all identify because all of us have done really ridiculous things.

Leslie: We've also learned to acknowledge the positive changes we see in one another, no matter how minor they may be. We say to each other: 'I respect and admire the changes that have been going on in your life.' A lot of times you see things that your friend doesn't have much perspective on. Of the three of us, I was the most dependent on men. I did many degrading things just to hang on to a man. I'm very healthy about men right now, and Rachel and Grace constantly reinforce the changes they've seen. I respect the fact that, whatever is going on with Grace's life in terms of men, it doesn't affect her self-esteem. She's able to look at it all as a growing experience.

I asked them how, based on their own experiences, people could support each other better.

Leslie: Gently point out the things they do that don't support them, such as sitting around complaining about their boyfriend or their boss or whatever. Gently show them it's not about other people; it's about them. I remember telling someone that in our group sessions we tell 'everything', and he responded, 'Boy, your boyfriend must hate that.' My boyfriend doesn't have a problem with it at all because we don't sit there and talk about him. It's about *our own behaviour*.

Rachel: I think friendship is about helping each other find solutions. To point out the positiveness in life, not to indulge in griping.

Another thing we can do to help each other is to
deemphasize the importance of looks. This issue has
bothered me for years. I was a model a while back,
and I felt like a prostitute because I was doing something I didn't believe in. I was saying, 'Buy these shorts
and you'll look like me.' Well, they wouldn't look like
me – and why would they want to? When I finally
pulled myself out of modelling, I went to the other
extreme. I wouldn't even wear make-up. I gained
weight. I didn't care about my hair. Now I've come
into a middle ground where I like the way I look.
People who know how I used to look as a model say,
'Why don't you dye your hair or wear more make-up
or whatever?' I always thought of myself as an intelligent woman. Now I look and act like an intelligent
woman, and that feels good. I think we are our own
enemies when we are focused on externals. I think we
need to reassure each other. I think we have to tell
our friends they look great the way they are, and that
they *are* great the way they are, regardless of their
looks.

Grace: Also, I think friends have to stop each other
from putting other people down. When I start talking
about other people negatively, I know something is
going on within me. I know I need some attention
that I am not giving myself or something like that. My
favourite thought is that if you run into one asshole
during the day, well, that's OK. It's a possibility. But if
you run into two, it's you that's the asshole . . . and
you'd better look at what's going on inside!

Rachel: We have learned to honour our commitments
to other women – which is a far cry from the times

we would break dates with our girlfriends to be with some guy! When I make a plan with a girlfriend, it is firm and I wouldn't let her down for anything. My husband is very supportive of that. I encourage him to see his male friends as well. Your partner sees you showing self-respect by honouring your women friends, and he respects you for that – that is, if he is a healthy man.

Leslie: I used to use jealousy and comparison as a way of beating myself over the head. Now I look at what other women have as inspiration, not competition. My first instinct is still, 'That bitch, everything is always perfect for her!' The jealousy pops out but I quickly jump into, 'I think that's wonderful. If she has that, it means I can have it too. There's room for all of us to have what we want.' And the thing is that I can now laugh about my bitchiness instead of getting hung up on self-criticism.

Grace: I think your relationships with people reflect how much you value yourself. If you nurture and support your relationship with women, it is a reflection of how you nurture and support yourself. And if you nurture and support your relationship with men, it's a reflection of the same thing. It's *all* the same thing. I'm constantly seeking that special connection with other people. Some people call it seeking God, or seeking a spiritual life, but I'm just seeking to feel close to other people. When I hit that connection, it makes me feel I really do belong – that I have a purpose here.

Three pretty fabulous women, indeed! Their growth warms my heart. To me their story demonstrates what friends can do for our lives that parents and lovers simply cannot. We all need friends. We all need each other.

Finally, it is important to recognize that, even though there are those among us who are incapable of showing their love for us, that love always exists. The following story that Steve, a lawyer, told me so beautifully demonstrates his understanding of how much we all yearn to share our deepest selves:

Jim has been my friend for about twenty-five years. He's very reserved, and anything I talk about beyond baseball, football and women he doesn't want to know. But about a year or so ago he had his third back operation, and it was really difficult. Two nights before he had the surgery, his wife called and said he was very down about it. I went over to the hospital and on the way bought about twenty or thirty bucks' worth of Chinese food and a paper tablecloth and napkins that said 'Happy Birthday' – it wasn't his birthday, but they were the only kind I could find – and I spread it all over his bed and we ate this Chinese food and had a ball. He had his surgery and everything was fine.

And then he sent me a card. (Now he has never written a card to me in twenty-five years!) It said, 'Dear Steve, I know we have been friends for all these years and I have always wanted to tell you something. I love you and thank you for all you've done for me.' I'll save that card till they bury me. Even now when I think about it I get really choked up. Because this is a guy that even to this day shows no emotion. So what I think is, this desire to communicate our love is really in everybody. It is really just a question of how you get it out, when you get it out, and who you get it out with.

8

Sharing the Deepest, the Darkest and the Dirtiest!

Two men's voices, talking about a place where their acts can be dropped, their masks can be shed, and a sense of belonging is created:

> 'I don't necessarily come for 'enlightenment'. I come for camaraderie one night, perhaps to share another night, or to hear someone else share, or whatever. There is a different kind of energy when you get us together this way – one of membership, belonging, commitment. It's really a marvellous kind of relating that is totally new to me.'

> 'Most men can't say 'I love you' to each other. They say it in different ways. I am not someone who communicates well, and I have friends who can't communicate well either, but we have a code. It was the same

growing up in my family. The love was there,
but it was masked in jokes or codewords or
something. But here, we don't use codewords. We learn to speak honestly, and it's
safe. The masks are ripped off here. We can
cry safely.'

Where is this wonderful place in which such connection is possible? It happens to be a men's self-help
group. These groups are growing quickly in the United
States and there are signs that they are catching on
in Europe and other countries as well. Women have
been gathering together in such groups ever since the
advent of the women's movement several decades ago,
and now it's time for men to enjoy the benefits too.

We can build our self-esteem by reading books,
listening to inspirational tapes, and doing our Higher
Self 'exercises'. But it takes human interaction in a
safe place to learn the language of openness which,
in a Somebody-Trained world, is a foreign language
indeed.

Too many of us don't have a clue as to what openness looks like, sounds like or feels like. We make
unsuccessful attempts at openness and are disheart-
ened by a dismal failure to connect. As a result, we
end up withdrawing even further into our feelings
of alienation. It is in the safety and support of the
group process that we can finally learn the language
of openness in a non-threatening way. We find out
that what we have been hiding beneath our act is
nothing to be ashamed of – rather, it is wonderfully
human. It is very healing to hear for ourselves that
the inner experiences of others are no different from
ours.

In the context of the group, we learn with great
relief that we are not bad, or ungrateful, or sick, or
alone, or warped, or lacking. We learn that our feelings are universally shared. In his seminars, psychologist Ken Druck sometimes asks participants not to
reveal their occupations when they introduce themselves. He says: 'I was surprised to learn that the inner
life of a carpenter is no different from that of a
surgeon.'[1] The group process proves that, despite outer
differences in our looks, careers, age, financial status,
gender or whatever, **feelings are the great connector.**
As feelings emerge, the walls of separation come
tumbling down and the 'empty suits' are soon filled
with beautiful human beings.

You may be someone who resists the group process.
You may be under the erroneous assumption that
people who attend groups are either 'crazies' or
'losers' who can't make it on their own. On the
contrary, they are comprised largely of people who
on the surface appear to be making it very successfully. And what motivates them to join a group is the
realization that their apparent 'success' has not
brought much happiness, fulfilment or satisfaction.
Some are straight business types who have 'made the
grade' yet know that something is missing in their
lives; some are new to parenthood, which brings up
many unresolved issues with their own parents; some
are frustrated with their inability to communicate with
members of the opposite sex. The reasons go on and
on. The group provides a safe arena in which they
can reveal the truth behind their acts. Ultimately, they
learn to take this truthfulness into the outside world
as well – to their partners, friends, children, parents
and workplace.

You may be resisting group participation because you believe that they are attended only by homosexuals. This, too, is untrue. While homosexual men and women have found tremendous value in meeting together in groups to heal their inner wounds; heterosexual men and women are now meeting together in huge numbers for the same purpose.

Or you may be resisting simply because you don't like the idea of opening up in front of a group of 'strangers'. Underlying your discomfort lies the fear of revealing what you consider 'bad' about yourself. It's an old throwback to the 'I don't like airing my dirty laundry in public' mentality, which translates as 'Part of me is dirty'. (That's your Somebody Training talking!)

> Once you understand the beauty of being 'real', you realize there is no such thing as dirty laundry when it comes to feelings.

So if you are resisting the idea of group participation, that's fine. Understand that it's only your fear talking – then, once again, 'feel the fear and do it anyway!'

This isn't to say that the group process is the only way to learn the language of openness. I do believe, however, that it can be the fastest and potentially most joyful. There are many types of groups to explore – therapist-led groups, self-help or self-awareness groups, and the Twelve-Step programme discussed in Chapter 3, to name a few. Each offers a wonderful 'classroom' for learning how to open up – without shame – to the truths we hold within.

Whatever kind of group you may choose, it is

important to choose wisely. The important question to ask yourself is this: 'Is the group based on Everybody Training or Somebody Training principles?' Here are a few guidelines to help you judge for yourself.

An Everybody Training group helps us to get in touch with our power

So the question to be asked is, 'Does the group foster a "victim" mentality or does it help you to take responsibility for your life?' If it is a breast-beating set-up, with everyone discussing each other's drama, this is not the group for you.

An Everybody Training Group uses such emotions as pain, anger and loneliness as tools of self-discovery

For example, a 'victim' question such as 'Why did she do that to me?' would not receive a 'victim' answer such as 'You poor thing. How could she be so terrible?' The response would be something like this: 'What do you think is beneath your feeling of upset?' or 'What can you do to stop that happening again?' In this way, the group's response turns a 'victim' into a 'creator' and in so doing, members of the group help each other to find the power within.

An Everybody Training group creates pride in our authentic self

If **judgment** plays a major role in the group, this is not the place for you. This isn't to say that we shouldn't be confronted with our 'acts', but in a loving, not critical, manner. Any group that creates more feelings of shame or inadequacy in its members is one to avoid.

An Everybody Training group is not hostile

While hostile emotions, even **verbal** fights, certainly do come up in group meetings, it should be a safe place for them to come up. When hostility arises, the group's job is simply, without judgment, to ask what's really going on beneath all the hostility. It doesn't take sides or pit one person against another. The group is there to serve as a neutral and compassionate observer. And, of course, physical violence in a group is never to be tolerated!

An Everybody Training group is spiritual in nature

The more we focus on our humanity and compassion in the group, the more we will feel at one with the world around us in our everyday activities.

You will feel awkward at the beginning. In any situation involving other people, it takes a while to feel a sense of belonging. But if, after four or five sessions, you still don't feel very good about being there, or feel abused in any way, follow your gut reaction and try another group.

Given these positive guidelines, the group setting offers a room of **'practice people'**. Here, we get to test out the new openness we are learning. Actual soul-friendships may or may not arise from the group. Remember that friendship is not the purpose of the group; rather, the purpose is to teach us how to open up, to share, to trust, to learn that we are not alone in our feelings, to feel at ease with our feelings, to diminish our need to impress others, to begin to love who we truly are. With this array of powerful teachings, it's then much easier to go out into the 'real' world and make those important one-to-one connections in all areas of our lives.

At the outset, there are advantages in attending same-sex groups. What we can learn – men with men and women with women – is the following . . .

1) To love our own sex (a surprising number of us don't!).

2) To find our inner power, which many women and men have lost along the way. (It is my feeling that men's violence towards women represents intense feelings of powerlessness and loneliness, and that the same feelings in women motivate the surprisingly large number of cases of violence against men.)

3) To pull ourselves away from the stifling roles that society has placed upon us, and discover who and what we truly want to be.

4) To become less dependent on, and therefore more truly loving towards, members of the opposite sex.

5) To get out our anger and grief in a less self-conscious environment.

6) To create a healthy sexual identification. (Most men have had few male role models when they

were growing up, and most women had models whom they didn't like very much).

There are a number of areas in which men need greater support than women, and vice versa. The 'privacy' of same-sex groups enables many of these issues to be worked through. Here are a few examples (these issues apply to both sexes, but are more pronounced in one sex than the other):

MEN'S ISSUES

One of the biggest barriers to men's openness with each other is the 'homosexual taboo'. Philosopher Sam Keen points out:

> 'After hearing of the loneliness of men in the course of my many years of leading groups, I have concluded that modern men avoid friendship with other men for fear that any tenderness might be a sign of homosexuality. We dare not touch each other, dare not allow the façade to slip, dare not confess that we are vulnerable, lonely, tired, not in control, that our relationships with women have not given us the intimacy we need, that we fear letting loose of our competitive relationships with each other.'[2]

This 'homosexual taboo' is not as much of an issue for women. Many more women than men feel comfortable walking arm in arm, hugging each other warmly, and crying on each other's shoulders without worrying about accusations of lesbianism. In the safety of a group, men can work through this homosexual taboo.

Another barrier to male friendship is men's intense discomfort in reaching out to one another when support is needed. This discomfort comes primarily from two sources. First, our Somebody Training has taught us that a 'real man' can go it alone. And second, men are taught to compete with, not support, one another. As a result many men suffer alone, which leads to all sorts of soul-destroying addictions, poor health and even suicide. Before shooting himself in the head, one man left a note which said simply, 'I had no one to talk to.'[3] This was in spite of the fact that he was a family man and had three 'buddies' with whom he went shooting on a regular basis.

Some men try turning to women for help, but the results can be very humiliating. While women claim they want open, sensitive men, many (though not all) withdraw when feelings which they consider 'weak' are actually revealed by their men. It is clear that the need for the 'strong, silent type' still exists for many women (as does the need for the 'obedient woman' for many men). Our tastes haven't yet caught up with the changing times.[4]

Another source of discomfort that men have in reaching out to other men has historical roots. At the time of the industrial revolution, it was decided that fathers should go off to work and leave the child-raising to the women. Like good soldiers, all the daddies marched out of the house, never to return as intimate companions and teachers to their children. And like good girls, all the mummies went along with it.

Poet Robert Bly, who leads men's groups across the USA, says that, as a result of fathers being absent during their sons' childhoods, a primary emotion in his groups is **grief**. 'Men of all ages . . . look back on their own lives and confront memories of fathers they never really knew.'[5] With no early male intimacy, boys grow up being very uncomfortable with emotion – man to man.

A fourth barrier to male friendships comes from the fact that, when their fathers went off to work, boys growing up not only grieved for their lost fathers but also lost touch with their masculinity. This sounds like a strange thing to say in a world where the pressure is on men to get in touch with their 'feminine' side. But it is now being recognized that men are out of touch not only with their feminine side but with their masculine side as well. This, of course, leaves them in the middle of nowhere.

In the context of a men's group, this lost 'masculinity' can be rediscovered – or, at least, a newer, healthier model can be created. What men have been portraying up until now with their macho stand is a pseudo-masculinity that has been imposed by a lost society comprised of weak and fearful men and women. Robert Bly suggests that a healthier kind of masculinity looks for 'a way to be powerful without being macho and a way to have feelings without feeling feminized'.[6] Men's groups help men find the way.

Given this history, the value of a men's group becomes evident. Here, often for the first time in front of other men, men can allow themselves to cry, to express their feelings of powerlessness and grief, and to be held and comforted. In so doing, they learn to see each other as a source of nurturance and are able to transform their relationship from one of rivalry to one of connection.

You can imagine how powerfully this change of perception can ultimately affect the ability to create soul-friendships outside the group. You can also imagine the relief when men finally realize that they don't have to go it alone. I believe that nowhere can men be shaken out of their intense isolation with more tenderness and compassion than in the 'womb' of a loving men's group.

WOMEN'S ISSUES

An important issue to be dealt with in a women's group has to do with the way women's expectations have been created according to the fairy tales they read as children. Men don't take so much account of these fairy tales. Perhaps that is because the Prince Charmings in these pseudo-lovely little stories always seem to get a bum deal! If you notice, they are always cast in the role of heroes (instead of mere humans) and are usually forced to put themselves at risk rescuing the damsel in distress, who always gets to be taken care of. While it doesn't do much for women's self-esteem, it is quite a seductive scenario. Who, at some level of their being – man or woman – doesn't yearn to be taken care of? In a group, women can create a more powerful 'fairy tale' which allows them to feel strong enough to take care of themselves, leaving them less dependent and more loving to men as a result.

Let's take poor old Cinderella as an example. In the original story, we find Cinderella and her step-mother and stepsisters in a terribly dysfunctional and co-dependent relationship. To make matters worse, Cinderella is a classic 'victim', totally refusing to take responsibility for her life as she drones day in and day out, 'Some day my prince will come.'

Enter a manipulative control freak – Cinderella's fairy godmother – who sets up a devious plan to fool the prince. Cinderella, having no backbone whatso-ever, goes along with this and rides off to the ball pretending to be something she definitely is not. Our young prince, fool that he is, is smitten and never looks beyond all the make-up. Cinderella, feeling very insecure (for good reason), disappears at the stroke of midnight, petrified that the prince will find out who she really is.

But never fear. Having delved into his past history, Cinderella's fairy godmother knew that the prince would be drawn to any women who played really hard to get. Our prince finally finds her via the famous glass slipper, only to discover she isn't quite the person she pretended to be. Nevertheless, he rides off with her into the sunset knowing in his heart that he can change her into anything he wants her to be – and we all know he is right! And if we tuned in twenty years later, we'd find Cinderella sitting around worrying that some young damsel with a smaller foot might lure her 'secu-rity blanket' away from her. Yuk!

Let's change the story into something much more powerful. How about this scenario? Cinderella goes along with the game plan until she arrives at the ball, then she realizes that what she is doing lacks integrity and she can't go on with the charade any longer. Determined to find a better way to get what she wants out of life, she turns to leave. The prince, smitten by her beauty, runs after her, but she tells him that she isn't ready for marriage; besides, they hardly know one another. She then goes home and packs her little bag, ignoring the guilt trip her stepmother and stepsisters are trying to lay on her. She kisses each one on the cheek, assuring them that they can all make it on their own, and as our tale ends we see Cinderella walking off into the sunrise to explore all the wonderful adventures life has to offer.

Some of you might prefer my sister's version. After Cinderella's stepmother and stepsisters go off to the ball, Cinderella decides that enough is enough and finally takes matters into her own hands. When her fairy godmother shows up and presents her devious plan, mice and all, Cinderella insists, 'Forget the prince and get me a locksmith instead!' Since the house was originally left to her by her father, she claims rightful ownership and changes all the locks on the door. Then off to the ball she goes, rags and all, to inform her stepmother and stepsisters that they are no longer welcome in her home. Undaunted by their cries of protest, she turns to leave. The prince, smitten by her fire and spirit, rushes after her, but, knowing his reputation as a spoiled brat, she informs him she isn't interested. 'And why are you wearing those funny pants?' she asks. Then she takes off, determined to make a life for herself, and wondering what all those silly women see in him anyway. Back home, she contacts the local council to get rid of all the mice and begins to redecorate her house the way she always wanted it to be. In the process, she makes a lot of friends who tell her she's really talented as a decorator and ought to go into the business. And so she does, very successfully. Ultimately, she finds a wonderful and supportive male business partner. They fall in love and live happily ever after . . . with her maintaining 51 per cent of the business.

Yes, a women's group can help rid us of our soul-destroying fantasies and allow us to explore healthier and much more exciting ways to go forward in life!

Another issue that can be dealt with in a women's group is our unhealthy preoccupation with appearance. Yes, men are concerned about their looks, but one only needs to glance at women's magazines or listen to their conversations to appreciate the depth of women's preoccupation with looks. Again, while some women blame men for wanting only those who are perfect, my experience, professionally and personally, is that men aren't half as concerned about our looks as we are – and some don't care at all. With the support of an Everybody Training women's group we can begin to understand that a preoccupation with our looks is destructive, and that beauty doesn't make our dreams come true.

A women's group can also help women kick the habit of blaming men for all the ills in the world. Everybody Training teaches us that there are really no enemies out there. Clearly, men have been just as badly damaged by our Somebody Training society as we have – they're just not as vocal about it. In any case, women need to support one another in taking charge of their lives and not allowing themselves to be taken advantage of in any way. As we realize that we have the power to control our experience of life, blame comes to serve no purpose . . . and what's left is the love.

A fourth issue for women is a very deep, sometimes repressed, feeling of being second-class citizens. Many women hide it well with their bravado, righteousness, judgment and anger, but the deep sense of inferiority that our Somebody Training society has tried to impose upon them has been clearly felt. As women learn to stand tall with one another, a new dignity and confidence about who they are will ultimately tip the balance. While men also feel inferior, our society is set up in a way that makes it harder for women to feel pride in themselves as a sex. Women can help each other bring out this self-respect.

'Co-ed' groups have advantages as well. Just as having friends of the opposite sex broadens our perspective, so does a mixed group. In fact, in the group situation you will discover more about the opposite sex than you ever could in a one-to-one friendship. It is here, in a room filled with 'practice people', that both sexes feel really safe in opening up. In a friendship there often is still an image to uphold, so openness can be difficult.

HOW TO CREATE YOUR OWN SELF-HELP GROUP

If you can't find a self-help group in your area, here's a crash course on starting one.

The first step is obviously to enlist members. Usually, a look through your address book and a few phone calls can start the ball rolling, and friends can help pass the word. You have to decide whether you want the group to be single-sexed or mixed. Each has distinct advantages. The only thing that everyone needs to have in common is an interest in growing as a human being.

Next you need to create a weekly format. Here is a sample. Remember that nothing is written in stone, and you and the other members of the group may find even better ways for creating the environment you want to create. Be flexible.

a) Each member puts his or her name on a slip of paper which is then put into a container. The name that is drawn from the container becomes the 'leader' for the week.

b) The leader for the week reads the statement of purpose that reminds everyone why they are there. For example:

'We have chosen to be here today for the purpose of reaching out and helping one another to grow into powerful and loving human beings. We are committed to coming from that part of ourselves that is filled with integrity and caring. We appreciate that we are all human beings doing the very best we can, and that through our mutual compassion we can learn to see the light within us all.'

Members of the group can create a circle, hold hands and close their eyes while the statement of purpose is being read. It is surprising how much 'closeness' this circle creates.

c) Begin the 'go-around', a warming-up period in which each member has a few minutes to say what has been happening to him or her during the week, or what he or she is feeling at that particular time.

d) Next the leader asks if anyone wants to 'work' – that is, to discuss with the group something that is going on in their lives, whether distressing or joyful. The key word is **sharing**. In the early stages of a group's history much of the talk that may go on is about 'story' ('She said to me . . . and I said to her'). But as the group begins to feel the safety of the room (which could take a long time for some), the feelings behind the stories begin to emerge. Be patient. For some very reserved people opening up takes an enormous amount of trust, and some will be able to share more than others.

e) This process is continued for the two or three hours that the meeting lasts. On some evenings not everyone has a chance (or desire) to 'work'. That's fine. They'll learn from what the others have to say. Eventually everyone understands that 'you are me and I am you', and in this way the basis of trust is formed.

One variation to get you started is to use as homework the exercises in a self-help book as suggested in Chapter 7. Then, use the group time to share the issues the assignments bring up. Many of my readers report great success in using the exercises in my books as the basis of their self-help groups; many other self-help books contain exercises as well.

Another variation is to have a theme for the week, which group members can discuss as it relates to their own lives. Some possible themes could be loneliness, dependency, anger, friendship, romance and fear.

f) When the three hours (or whatever time frame you have decided upon) is over, it is wonderful for group members to go around the room thanking each other for being there, preferably with a hug.

g) You may decide to create a system whereby each member is assigned a 'growth partner' in the group, with whom he or she can connect throughout the week to offer support or talk through any problems.

It's helpful to keep to the time limits allotted, as without them the conversation wanders. Naturally there will be occasions when extra time is needed, if someone is dealing with a heavy issue.

It is important to incorporate the guidelines for an Everybody-Trained group as discussed earlier in the chapter. The essential principle is not to fall into a complaining or victim mode of interacting. Rather, the objective is to enable group members to take responsibility for their lives and to change what doesn't seem to be working for them.

There are other possible formats. For example, one men's group always starts with a pot-luck dinner, as they feel that 'breaking bread together' helps break the ice. Everyone brings whatever food they want to bring, and sometimes it's a real mishmash, but they don't care. They put it all out on the table with paper plates and cups, and for an hour they eat and wind down from the pressures of the day. (Naturally, no alcohol or other drugs are allowed.) Then they're ready to begin.

A few extra tips:

Allow absolutely no physical violence

It is true that conflict often develops in a group session; it's a natural and important part of growth. But this rule must be applied: **if anyone tries to commit physical violence, he or she is out of the group**. If verbal conflict becomes too heated, the group leader steps in and mediates. The group can also step in and ask each person involved in the verbal conflict what is 'really' going on beneath the anger. Much personal insight is gained in this way.

Don't be upset if some members drop out

The groups that have been meeting for long periods of time usually have a core group around which other members come and go. Some stay until they've got all they can from the group in terms of growth; others, finding it is 'not for them', leave after one or two meetings. Some group members attend only sporadically. This is also to be expected. As time goes by, you will find your bonding occurs mostly between the regulars.

A group doesn't have to last forever

If after a few months a group dissipates, that's fine. Even a short-term experience is valuable, though you may want to join or create another group.

Commitment allows greater growth

Those who get the most out of a group are those who honour its verbal or non-verbal contracts. Commitment means being there regularly, being there on time, and being there when someone needs you. If you show up at meetings only when *you* need to share a particular problem, that's fine, but true connection comes when you are also there to help others. Otherwise you will never achieve a sense of participation and importance in the human family.

It suggests that you don't value yourself enough to feel of value to someone else. And the truth is that you really are important.

Don't judge how others use the group

If you are committed to the group, it may upset you if someone is less so – that is, if they habitually come late or sporadically, or whatever. Understand that everyone has a different agenda. The key is to take responsibility for yourself and not to judge anyone else. If this is difficult, notice your self-righteousness and work on letting people do what is right for them. Just take the attitude that 'Whatever anyone does, it's fine. I'm going to get from and give to whoever is there.'

Expect an initial learning process during which all does not go as planned

In a novice group, mistakes are to be expected and learned from. For example, it is scary being the leader for the first time, and the chosen leader may not hold in the reins tightly enough. Members of the group can guide each other and learn from one another. Flexibility is the key. Change what doesn't work, and keep the rest.

Take responsibility for your experiences in a group

If you don't agree with something, *speak up*. This may be hard in the beginning, but as you feel more comfortable your courage will increase. Remember that it is helpful to everyone if you tell what is true for you. **Also, if membership of the group brings up things that are too difficult for you to handle, seek professional help immediately, which leads me to . . .**

Self-help groups are not therapy

If a group member appears to be embroiled in an overwhelming emotional problem, it is important that the group encourages him or her to seek therapy. One man recalled:

> 'I had a tough time in 1988, and it seemed that for a while everybody in the group was dealing with my depression. I would be silent and the guys would try to pull me out of it, and I started to feel ashamed that I was always depressed. Finally one of the guys said, 'You need more than we can give you. You have to go to therapy.' They made me see that I was using the group to avoid the real confrontation with my pain that is best dealt with in therapy. They really pushed me into getting proper help. And I went to a therapist who pulled me out of my depression.'

THERAPIST-LED GROUPS

You may wonder if therapist-led groups are more valuable than self-help groups. In some ways, yes. A therapist skilled in the group process can get the group to open up to each other more quickly. He or she can also avoid some of the early pitfalls that a novice group may fall into. Further, he or she is better equipped than group members to lead the group into meaningful insights. Most importantly, contrary to a self-help group, a therapist-led group can obviously get into the realms of therapy, which can be very valuable. The downside is that therapist-led groups can be expensive if attended regularly, as they should be. They are also dependent on the therapist. I know of self-help groups that have been meeting for over ten years. Since they have no leaders, they are self-sufficient and depend only on the willingness of members to show up.

If you decide to try a therapist-led group, it is important to choose a therapist who leads groups with an Everybody Training perspective, as described earlier in the chapter. It is also helpful when therapists do not portray themselves as 'perfect people', but instead share their own foibles.

While both types of groups – self-help and therapist-led – differ in a number of respects, I believe that a tremendous amount of value can be gained from both. I have been a member of both types of groups and they each have played an important role on my journey toward self-discovery, wholeness and connection.

INTENSIVE WORKSHOPS

I also recommend intensive workshops in addition to (not instead of) an on-going self-help or therapist-led group. The intensive workshops I have attended lasted anywhere from a weekend to one week. Some are longer. They are usually structured in a way that allows emotional break-throughs to happen within a very short period of time. If you have ever attended weekend workshops you will have watched people arrive with their walls built up, but very quickly drop their acts and become real.

Intensive workshops allow us to run the gamut of emotions and are often *verbally* very confrontational at the beginning. But no matter what kind of intensive workshop I've attended, they have always ended up on the kind of loving note that is seldom possible to obtain in our everyday world. I couldn't describe it any better than author and teacher Alan Cohen as he talks rhapsodically about the last evening of a weekend workshop he attended:

> 'By Sunday afternoon something happens, something which I cannot really explain, a rare, even miraculous event that reminds me that life is indeed precious, worth living. It is the merging of twelve half-empty human beings into one whole, living, loving, spiritually-endowed Force. It is the birth of the soul into joyous expression, the transformation of Children of God from slumber to aliveness, and the fulfillment of the prayer, "on earth as it is in heaven . . .". I remember one such group of us sitting in our circle on Sunday afternoon, and I tell you it felt as if there was just one big bathtub of love in that room, a universal womb that we all shared.'[7]

Yes, well-led intensive workshops are indeed capable of creating a feeling of heaven on earth. I speak from experience. Even if the feeling of sublime connection is only for a brief moment in time, once we have the experience of what is possible in terms of human connection we are eager to follow the path that leads to a greater opening of our hearts and souls to one another. It feels so good.

Where do you find intensive workshops? Details can usually be found on the internet, in local papers or on noticeboards in New Age-type bookshops, health food shops or public libraries. The best way of finding an intensive workshop is to mention your desire to attend one to everyone you know. Also write off to the useful addresses that are found at the end of many self-help books. Soon you will be getting announcements of workshops happening all over the place! (If you are in therapy, consult your therapist if you are planning to attend a self-help group or an intensive workshop.)

For those of you who are sceptical or frightened about the group process, here are some first-hand accounts. The core of this American men's group has been meeting every Thursday night for approximately five years. There are twenty-seven members now, of which ten to fifteen show up at each meeting. Their ages range from the twenties into the sixties. They are all heterosexual. Some are married, some divorced, while some have never been married. Their backgrounds, careers, financial status and personalities differ, but they come together every Thursday night to share the experience that is common to all of them – growing up male in our Somebody-Trained society. I asked the men to share with me (and you) what the group has meant to them. Here are some of their answers:

'I have been willing to risk openness with other men because of my experience in the group. The reason for this is that I've really learned here that the bottom line is we're all the same anyway. So, even though someone may be closed to you outside the group, you have to assume that if he were in this group he would be more or less the same. So, I'm much more open out there.'

'The group really has helped me see *into* a man instead of only looking at him. Take Jack. When I first met him I thought this is one macho guy. Good-looking. A beautiful wife. Corvette. And he lives in Malibu. When I got to know Jack better, I realized his macho stuff was a mask, just his way of coping. I've touched enough of his insides to know this is a man who hurts like I do; he can cry; he can feel lonely. So he is no different than the next guy. And if that is the case, then we are all going through this together. And I can relate to the stranger out there in the same way. In this way, I don't feel inferior to someone who appears to have more and I don't feel superior to someone who appears to have less. We're really all the same.'

'What the group gives me is safety and constructive feedback when I screw up. We have formed an alliance here that feels very comfortable and very strong. I used to be really unsure of myself with other men, but slowly, as I learn to feel more powerful, I'm learning to communicate 'out there' as well.'

'Until I met this group, I relied on women as friends. Now I feel a real bonding with men as well.'

'I always had a buddy when I was growing up. After I got married I stopped the buddy system and my wife became my buddy. After I got divorced women became my buddies.

And then one day I realized that I was not cultivating any male friendships. I had got out of my male buddy system. And in my own inner journey I recognized I needed some deeper communication with a man or men.'

'I have never felt a physical connection with men. But here we hug and it feels OK. It's all out of our own bonding together . . . out of our love for each other.'

'Out in the world, most men will do anything to protect their image. You can't appear vulnerable, and that probably goes back to life in caves 65 million years ago. It's only when you get into a group like this that you can leave your image outside and really talk about what we feel and what we are.'

'It's still hard for me to reveal a lot of who I am, even though I'm in the group. If I'm not sure of myself, I let it pass. I'm still not comfortable sharing certain things about myself that would make me look like less of a man. But I'm learning.'

'My parents were very judgmental and expected perfection. I always wondered, 'Is there any-one who will accept me as I am?' And then there was Jacob, my first friend ever. We just climbed trees, jumped up and down, dug holes, played with marbles and bottle caps, planned a war against the other guys next door, laughed together, and so on. I really loved this guy. Jacob became my link to my genuine self. He was the first person who allowed me integrity and self-acceptance. And this happened at age five. I haven't seen him since I was nine years old and I've never had a friend like that again. This group is the closest I've come.'

'You know, something has happened to my definition of "strength" since I have been in this group. I used to think macho was strength, but now I realize that it is the courage to open up and be vulnerable. I am in awe of someone who has the courage to say, "I am just really feeling sad and naked right now." I think it really takes a lot. And I have seen, as some of us have shared at different times, that everybody has the same thing. They, too, feel embarrassment. They, too, feel shame. And I've learned that one can have all that and still be strong.'

'I had close friends in high school but not for the fifteen years since. I began to see in this group that really deep relationships were possible in adulthood. As a result, my relationships have become much deeper out there. In fact, I've become "demanding" with those I spend time with. I don't want to hang out with anyone and take time away from my family unless I can have that depth of connection. I've seen what quality is in here, and I want that same quality in other relationships,

whether it be with a man or a woman, stock-
broker or doctor.'

I asked how they would describe their relationships
with other men in the group. The consensus was:

> 'Friendships are formed in this group, but
> this is not a friendship group. We respect
> each other tremendously. We like each other
> and sometimes we become friends. But a lot
> of us will never be friends in the usual sense.
> We won't go out and do things together
> except on a planned group activity or retreat.
> I think we connect at a whole different level
> in here than with "friends" out there. It's
> more of a "bonding" than a friendship in
> the traditional sense. And yet I certainly feel
> that in a moment of need, if I had to get
> three or four guys on the phone, I probably
> could and I'd probably get the support I
> need. Yet, we might not see each other on a
> social level.'

I asked for any especially significant moments in the
group.

> 'We went on a five-day group outing to Jim's
> ranch in the country. One afternoon,
> someone suggested we play baseball.
> Throughout my schooldays I was always the
> last one to be picked when it came to base-
> ball. Each team tried to push me off on to
> the other team. I was so ashamed of that. I
> have been very thankful that as an adult I

never had to face baseball again. And here are all my group buddies saying, 'Let's play baseball!' I felt, 'Oh, my God!' and voiced my embarrassment to a couple of friends around me, one of whom volunteered to be a team captain. As he opened his mouth to pick his first team member, I heard him call my name *first*! And it was just so powerful to me. I don't remember if, when or where I hit the ball, but it didn't matter. I knew their eyes weren't there to judge me. I've carried this experience into so many things in my life. If ever I feel embarrassed or ashamed, I remind myself, 'Hey, you're an OK person and it really doesn't matter.' And I'm able to let it go. What an incredible impact that day had on me.'

'What has been very special to me are the moments when we've allowed ourselves to be just silly. I think people have forgotten or are ashamed of just being silly. For example, at Jim's ranch all of us went into the pond and there was nothing but black mud and slime on the bottom. I remember Tom started putting mud on everyone and we all joined in. And here we were – a dozen men, all totally covered in this black muck. And we were howling with laughter. God, that felt good.'

'I think one of the greatest things that happened in the group session was the night when I casually asked everyone what was their greatest fear, and we went round the room telling our fears. You really had to dig in. I know I was sweating when I was admitting mine. A lot of the guys had the same fears. And a lot of them were different. That was one of the most powerful evenings that I have ever spent.'

'One of the most amazing evenings for me was the night we talked about homosexuality. Someone started putting down gays and someone else defended them. It was getting kind of heated and someone finally said, 'OK, let's go round the room and each guy tell if he ever had a homosexual thought or experience or not.' And then each of us in turn revealed intimate thoughts or experiences in our childhood and adolescence that could be construed as homosexual. To me that was tremendously revealing about the openness of the group – to admit the truth to a group of heterosexual men and not fear being judged about something like that. I can't imagine a group of men under any other circumstances coming forward the way we did with humour, sincerity and understanding of our earlier experiences, and then simply letting it all go.'

'One night we went around the room and shared our most degrading sexual experience. When we realized that we all live with nightmares about the inability to perform, it was a big relief.'

'When the group first started up we heard a lot of words, but not so much feeling. For myself, I remember the evening that I was able openly to express my hurt about something that was going on in my life. That was an important moment for me. It wasn't easily done, and it took a lot of trust in myself and everyone here. But it was the first time I had been able to talk to anyone about the hurt I felt inside. I will always be indebted to the group for that.'

'I had an experience that was so powerful that I have yet to grasp the full significance of it. I joined the group three days after my wife left me. I had not eaten anything or slept since she had left. The group started to chit-chat about all sorts of things, and I realized I had to talk or I'd explode. I said, 'I have to tell you what happened', and I just completely broke down. I don't know if the group had ever devoted one whole meeting to one person before. But the whole group was there to help me heal. It was the most incredible thing that I could ever have experienced. Seven months have passed and I've gone from someone who saw absolutely no purpose in living to someone who can now stand up and say that life is great. But what the people here did for me – people who at the time barely knew me – is remarkable. They could feel I was really dying that evening. And that was the night when everybody reached out and didn't let somebody die. So when people in here say, 'If I am ever in trouble I know I have people here to help me,' God, I know it's true.'

These men and women who have expressed their feelings in this chapter have already learned one great lesson in life: that their lives make a difference and that they can, by sharing who they are, touch the lives of everyone around them.

9

Welcoming the Heart into the Workplace

Note: Even if you don't work at a job, don't skip this chapter. All the concepts and exercises described here can be applied to other areas of your life.

From the lowest job in the hierarchy to the highest, insecurity reigns as we bring into the workplace all the fears of our Everybody Training childhood.

'Am I good enough to make it out here?'
'Is my assistant after my job?'
'What if I get fired?'
'Does the boss like me?'
'Does she make more money than I do?'
'Will I be passed over when the next promotion comes up?'

Where there is insecurity, there is competition. Mum and Dad have laid the groundwork long before with 'Let's see who can be the first one ready for bed!' In so doing, they unwittingly create a situation where one child ends up feeling smugly triumphant while the other nurses his or her wounds of defeat. And then we wonder why there is so much sibling rivalry. And so it goes on ... through primary school, secondary school, college and then into the workplace. All our lives we have been given the underlying message: 'Be the best!' You may be saying to yourself, 'Come now, there's nothing wrong with a little healthy competition.' But, as you'll see, it is highly debatable whether such a thing as 'healthy' competition even exists.

The alienating wall that is created by competition is evident in all areas of our lives, but it is most visible in the world of work. The reason for this, as Ram Dass points out, is that wherever money and power are key, everyone, by definition, becomes a 'them' rather than an 'us'![1]

- If you are the boss, those lower in the hierarchy are a **them** because they might steal your job.
- If you have a boss, then he or she is a **them** because he or she may fire you.
- Your colleagues are a **them** because they may get ahead of you.
- Other companies are a **them** because they may steal your business, thereby taking money out of your pocket.
- Your friends are a **them** because they might become bigger Somebodies than you are.
- People of the opposite sex or different ethnic background, age, appearance or whatever become a **them** because they may take the job that you feel rightfully should be yours.
- Even your family becomes a **them**, because they don't understand why you are not making more

Dare to Connect

money and/or why you work so many hours and do not spend enough time with them.

How can there be anything but a sense of separateness in such a fearful structure? The question is this: Is it possible to transform the Somebody Training practices, which create separation in the workplace, to the Everybody Training practices, which create connection?

I strongly believe that it is. In fact, as I look around I see transformation on its way, like a wave beginning its roll in to the shore. I don't think we could stop it if we tried. After what seems to have been a very long and very deep sleep, people all over the world are waking up to the fact that our traditional, competitive mode no longer works. Job satisfaction is rare, people consumed with getting ahead are doing so at the expense of personal relationships, and the place we call home – our planet – is being destroyed right before our eyes. Because it's become virtually impossible to avoid all this bad news, people are beginning to take notice, and, as a result, a new work ethic is clearly on the horizon. And its central unifying ingredient is clearly **connection** rather than the 'everyman-for-himself' doctrine that has ruled up until now.

I'd like to suggest some powerful ways that each and every one of us can make a difference in helping to make the world of work one of connection rather than competition. I know that one often feels powerless when facing a huge system that seems to be locked into old ways of thinking. Yet there really is much that we, as individuals, can do to create change in our own unique way – whether we are in the mail room or are the chief executive officer of a major corporation, or own our own business; whether we are a teacher, construction worker, lawyer or secretary, or whether we work at home.

I love the following story told by researcher and author Amy Domini at a business conference held in New York. A little girl goes out after a storm to throw back some starfish that have become stranded on the beach. Told there are too many starfish for her to make any difference, she says, as she throws one back, 'I made a difference to that one, didn't I?'[2] So can you.

Notice areas at work in which you can personally be responsible for changing an attitude of alienation to one of healthy connection. You will be surprised at how creative you can be when connection (outflow) is the motivation instead of competition (fear), and how you can help turn a 'dog-eat-dog' mentality into an 'everybody-can-win' mentality that will warm the world around you. Here are some guidelines:

EXPAND THE BOTTOM LINE

The 'bottom line' is a very important concept in business, signifying the particular end that justifies *all* the means. If you ask most people to identify what is presently the bottom line in the world of work, they would most probably answer:

Getting ahead.

This, of course, is a shortened version of . . .

Getting ahead (usually of someone else), in terms of profit, status and/or power.

Not great for connection! But what if we did a little mental magic and expanded our bottom line to look like this:

Getting Ahead

+

Caring About Colleagues

As we add a Higher Self dimension to our bottom line, our purpose is greatly expanded. We begin to bridge the gap with our colleagues as we start to see them as people *just like us*, people who would welcome our caring and consideration.

You may ask, 'Aren't "getting ahead" and "caring about colleagues" conflicting concepts?' Not necessarily. One can be promoted, yet with a sense of humanity instead of smug superiority. The former brings good wishes for success, while the latter brings disdain. Attitude makes a huge difference in our ability to connect with our colleagues.

The actions and attitudes that come from the narrow bottom line of **getting ahead** are very different from those that come from the expanded bottom line of **getting ahead + caring about colleagues**. The former strengthens the walls of alienation, while the latter strengthens the bonds of connection. **You or me** is soon replaced by **you and me**. With this expansion of our vision, we begin asking ourselves questions such as the following:

- Am I a positive force in this office (factory, school, home, or whatever)?

- Do I help people feel good about themselves by building them up, or do I pull them down by being judgmental and critical?
- Do I offer my help to those who could use it, or do I withhold it out of fear that they may get ahead of me?
- Am I a **taker**, or do **I give** a lot to those around me?
- Do I show genuine interest in the lives of my colleagues, or do I act as if I couldn't care less?

As we answer these questions truthfully, we can begin to move in the direction of connection instead of alienation. We can begin doing things that push our loving – instead of competitive – energy out towards the people around us and immediately begin healing the wounds that fear and competition always create. Can you see how this expansion of the bottom line can make the job so much more interesting?

In one of my workshops, I instructed all my students to try expanding the bottom line and participating full-out in their jobs for one entire week. I asked them to 'act-as-if' their actions really made a difference to everyone around them. The key question they were to ask themselves during the week was:

> 'If I were really important here, what would
> I be doing?'

And then they were to set about doing it.

Peggy resisted the assignment. She lamented that she hated her job in a public relations firm and was just biding her time until she found a new one. Each day was pure drudgery as she watched the clock move slowly through the eight painful hours. With great scepticism she finally agreed to try it for just one week, to expand her bottom line and commit herself 100 per cent to her job, knowing that she really counted.

The following week, as I watched Peggy walk into the room, I couldn't believe the difference in her energy level. With excitement in her voice, she reported the events of her week:

> 'My first step was to brighten up the dismal office with some plants and posters. I then started really to pay attention to the people I work with. If someone seemed unhappy, I asked if there was anything wrong and if I could help. If I went out for coffee, I always asked if there was anything I could bring back for the others. I complimented people. I invited two people for lunch. I told the boss something wonderful about one of my colleagues. (Usually I'm selling *myself*!)
>
> 'Then I asked myself how I could improve things for the company itself. First I stopped complaining about the job – I realized I was such a nag! I became a self-starter and came up with a few very good ideas which I began implementing. Every day I made a list of things I wanted to accomplish and I set about accomplishing them. I was really surprised by how much I could do in a day when I focused on what I was doing! I also noticed how fast the day goes by when I am involved. I put a sign on my desk that said, 'If I were really important here, what would I be doing?' And

> every time I started to fall back into my old patterns of boredom and complaining, the sign reminded me what I was supposed to be doing. That really helped.'

What a difference a simple expansion of the bottom line made in just one short week! It made Peggy feel connected to everyone and everything around her – including the organization itself.

It's important to note that her commitment didn't mean she had to stay at this job forever; it only meant that while she was there it was in everyone's best interest, particularly her own, to create a caring environment. Who wants to spend their days in a milieu filled with alienation, boredom and negativity? It is also worth noting that with such positive energy the likelihood of Peggy getting a great reference and finding a new, more challenging job would be greatly increased.

Now let's try expanding the bottom line even further to include still another Higher Self dimension:

Getting Ahead

+

Caring About Colleagues

+

Caring About the Community and Planet

Now our actions and attitudes have even more far reaching and exciting consequences. We are now paying attention to the fact that what we do affects the community we serve and the planet on which we live. Now we begin to ask ourselves some soul-searching questions, such as:

- Am I careless and shoddy in my job performance, thereby possibly causing people 'out there' distress and/or harm?
- Is the company I am working for (or own) helping humanity or hurting it in any way?
- If so, what can I do to change what is not humane?

We now begin considering the **quality** of our work as it relates to the ultimate consumers. We see that what we do makes a difference to someone out there. We also consider the **purpose** of our work and how it affects our planet, realizing we are connected to it all.

The two goals of **getting ahead** and **caring about the community and the planet** may conflict, and some changes may be the result. It may mean we have to leave a company which manufactures or markets products that we feel are harmful to consumers and the environment. One individual who made such a choice is Don Marrs, who was a very successful vice-president of a large advertising firm.[3] But there came a time when he looked around at what he was selling and got a knot in his stomach. He realized that the most exciting and lucrative accounts to work on were cigarettes, soft drinks, cereals with sugar, and oil companies that were irresponsible with the environment – all accounts that he believed were negative in some way. He talks of the enormous sense of release when he severed his attachments: 'I felt an exhilarating sense of freedom from the intolerable weight of having to support values that were no longer my own.'

Naturally, it isn't always necessary to change our careers or the companies we work for. A different choice would be to stay where we are and see if a difference could be made from within. But, whatever our choice,

> When our bottom line is expanded to include our colleagues, the community and the planet, our sense of alienation is greatly diminished as we realize that we truly are a meaningful part of it all.

Are you beginning to see the advantages?

- **As we expand the bottom line**, we become much more than we thought we were.
- **As we expand the bottom line**, we bring in the human values of **integrity** and **humanity**, which raises our self-esteem.
- **As we expand the bottom line**, the money, status and power lose some of their initial importance, and fear diminishes as we realize that who we are encompasses more than simply winning the race; it also encompasses the notion that we are caring human beings.
- **As we expand the bottom line**, our vision is enlarged to the point where we can see how we are all powerfully connected.
- **As we expand the bottom line**, we become less attached to our role. We realize that we may be the boss, the secretary or the boy in the mail room . . . **BUT WE ARE MORE**. We are all human beings who touch each other's lives.

And as we detach ourselves from our role, we find the risks are not so great. We don't get so lost in the drama of needing to be important; **WE ARE ALREADY**

IMPORTANT. We don't have to prove ourselves to anyone; **WE ARE ALREADY GOOD ENOUGH**. If we lose our job for any reason, we haven't lost our 'being-ness'; we know we are much more than our job, so we don't get depressed, scared and angry. Well, perhaps for a little while! But then we pull ourselves together and simply move forward in search of our next adventure in the world of work.

We still strive (perhaps even harder) to do our very best, but our attachment to the outcome diminishes. And new, more enlivening priorities step in to replace these limiting attachments. Of course, we need money. But,

> With an expanded bottom line, our identity
> is not dependent on being the leader of the
> pack. It is more dependent on how much
> love we are putting out into this world.

In this light, **getting ahead** is associated with meaningful connection rather than desperate neediness. So now we have a truly winning formula:

**Getting Ahead
(now with
integrity and
humanity)**
+
**Caring About   =   A Feeling of
Colleagues   Connection in the
                            Workplace**
+
**Caring About the
Community and
Planet**

Naturally, we can continue expanding our bottom line to include more personal dimensions such as **creating more balance in our lives, loving the work we do** and so on. But in terms of connection, the winning formula above will go a long way towards healing the wounds of separation.

As an exercise, I suggest that you sit down with pen and paper and make three 'to do' lists as you answer each of the following questions:

'What actions can I take to show my colleagues that I care about them?'

'What actions can I take to ensure that the community and the planet are well served?'

'How can I integrate the above with **getting ahead,** so that it is a win-win situation for everyone?'

Take the time to answer these questions in depth. When you think you've gone as far as you can go, think some more; you've only scratched the surface. And when you think you've *really* gone as far as you could go, think some more again. You'll be amazed at how creative you can become if you hang in there long enough!

Depending on your situation, you may want to invite some of your colleagues to join with you in the process. Set up an evening of sharing your ideas and seeing where you can interact with one another to reach some common goals.

As you begin the task of expanding the bottom line, you may experience a feeling of fear creeping in. Your internal Chatterbox will probably pop up a hundred times to tell you that the dog-eat-dog game is the only way to survive. You can tell that child-like little voice of yours not to worry – you're on the right path. The confusion and hesitation will soon pass as you exchange a destructive pattern of alienation and fear for a compassionate and life-enhancing one.

LEARN SOME OF THE WISDOM OF AIKIDO[4]

It is strange to think of a martial art as a means of connection, but Aikido is extremely healing in its principles. It teaches us about being strong without ever harming someone who is in conflict with us. Aikido has been translated as 'the way of blending energy' or 'a harmony of spirit and body'. Isn't that a wonderful way to begin to look at the world of work?

Three principles which I find especially meaningful as a way of living from our Higher Self in the world of work (and elsewhere) are as follows:

a) Don't fight, don't flee . . . just flow

This means that the alternative to either meeting the 'enemy' with force or simply giving up is to become a channel for the flow of positive energy. A practical way of using this concept is to visualize flowing out from our body a stream of energy that is filled with love, caring, compassion and connection, particularly when we're confronted with a difficult situation. In so doing we use the **flow** instead of the **fist** to create harmony in the midst of conflict.

When I find myself resisting what's going on around me, and thus blocking any resolution, I imagine myself as a gently rolling sea and let myself relax physically and mentally and flow with the situation. As I do this, I keep silently repeating one of my favourite affirmations:

I let go and trust it's all happening perfectly.

In a short time, I actually feel myself flowing instead of resisting. It is an amazingly powerful way to be in this world.

b) Extending *ki*

The world of science has discovered that we don't end where our skin does. In fact, a field of energy extends beyond our body and affects everything and everyone around us. Kirlean photography can actually capture this field on film as a body of light surrounding the body. Our physical, mental and spiritual state determine the 'health' of that body of light around our physical body. It can be negative and limited, or positive and expansive.

This energy field is called *ki* in Japan and *chi* in China. Most of us have little understanding of the potential power of our energy field – but powerful it certainly is! For example, when we are positive and expansive these qualities are radiated out through our physical body into our energy field, and we are treated in a far more positive and expansive manner than when our energy flow is negative and constricted. Always remember that energy attracts like energy . . . the Law of Attraction in action.

If you look back at the basics of connection in

Chapter 5, they can all be seen as an expansion of our *ki*; their purpose is to encompass rather than to alienate those 'strangers' in the room. The same can be said of Peggy's new behaviour, as described earlier in this chapter. As you learn how to expand your sphere of connectedness, you discover a wonderful ability to heal the alienation in the world of work and everywhere else in life. Without it, we tend to remain the victim who either fights or flees, but never flows.

c) Centring

Many of us have seen and heard the phrase 'getting centred' in recent self-help books and tapes, but what does it really mean? In *Feel the Fear and Do It Anyway* I explained how to centre by aligning the Higher Self, the conscious and the subconscious mind.[5] In Aikido, centring is similarly defined as the act of achieving balance between Body, Mind and Soul. If any one of these three components is off-balance, life doesn't flow very easily. And it is interesting that by balancing one, such as the physical, the other two are more likely to come into balance as well. The philosophy and practice of Aikido involve many centring exercises, and again I invite you to explore them.

It is important for you to understand that:

> Since we have all been students of the Somebody Training curriculum, we are, by definition, off-balance and uncentred.

This is so because we're always looking for external approval instead of focusing on our inner resources. This means that we can be knocked over very easily –

literally or figuratively. In addition, we are constantly distorting our very essence by trying to become something different from what we truly are.

When we learn to ground ourselves from within, and when we come from the place of flowing harmony between our Body, Mind and Soul, there is very little, if anything, that can topple us. We are whole, complete, at peace, and our vision is clear as we begin seeing through our own eyes instead of those of everyone around us.

Let me give you an example of how I use a version of all three of these concepts – flow, extending *ki* and centring – when facing what one study reported to be the number one fear in the USA (as it no doubt is in other countries too) – public speaking. (In this same study, fear of death was number seven – it seems we'd rather die than make a fool of ourselves!) Are you future public speakers ready?

1) Before I approach the stage, I find a way of looking at the faces in my audience from wherever I am sitting or standing.
2) As I scan the many 'strangers' in the audience, I 'extend *ki*' by silently repeating over and over again, 'I love you. I love you. I love you. I love you.' I know it sounds corny, but, believe me, as I do this my nervousness starts to melt away and I begin to feel a loving connection with the audience.
3) Once I have been introduced, I walk up on to the stage and I consciously centre myself, 'feeling' my feet planted firmly on the ground with roots going down into the earth. As I do this I visualize myself aligned with my Higher Self, and

remind myself that my only purpose is to give love.

4) I then imagine a ray of light emerging from above, filling my being with light, flowing into the room and surrounding everyone sitting before me. These last two steps sound rather time-consuming, but take only a few seconds.

5) If statements or questions from the audience express disagreement with me, I simply imagine the dialogue as part of the back-and-forth 'play' of people learning and growing together – 'the way of blending energy'. The alternative, rigid defensiveness, only creates alienation and tension in the room.

I cannot describe the high I get when I connect with my audience from that place of love and sharing. This is in stark contrast to those days when my knees knocked, my heart pounded and I was petrified that I wouldn't do a good job. Those were the days when I was only concerned about what I was going to **get** – such as praise, applause or good marks. When I extend my *ki* into my audience now, I am focused on the **giving**. When we are focused on the giving instead of the getting, our fear is transformed into an appreciation of the opportunity of sharing who we are with others.

This simple technique can be used in an interview, a meeting, the office or anywhere. Yes, even when approaching a bunch of uptight business types walled in by alienation we can be a healing force by simply projecting an '**I Love You**' or '**I Greet the Light In You**' energy into the room. If you can hold on to that loving space, the outcomes of meetings will be very different from those when our energy field broadcasts 'I am scared, insecure and I want desperately for you to love and accept **ME!**' Whenever we approach any situation in a centred state, extending our field of energy and light, we become more powerful and loving, rather than fearful and vulnerable.

This is a small taste of the richness of the principles of Aikido. I hope it whets your appetite enough to encourage you to explore further.

TRANSFORM COMPETITION INTO PARTNERSHIP

Competition is so inbred in the Western system of business that it is hard to believe it could be profitable any other way. On the surface, it seems to be true that without competition there can be no success. But those who have looked a little deeper have come up with a very different conclusion.

In many recent studies, the results surprisingly suggest that the **less** competitive one feels, the **more** one will succeed! Among other things, competition creates great anxiety and a limited perspective, which diminish performance considerably.

Alfie Kohn wrote a most enlightening book called *No Contest: The Case Against Competition.*[6] In all his extensive research, nowhere was he able to find evidence that competition had value. In fact, he found compelling evidence that competition is toxic, not only to the job, but also to the soul. He shows us how competition:

Poisons relationships

Makes us suspicious, hostile, envious, and contemptuous of losers

Destroys our self-esteem

Creates anxiety and need for approval

Is inefficient

Undermines genuine love of learning by focusing on external gain

Kills curiosity.

He describes competition as an 'against-ing' process. When asked if competition caused aggression, he responds, **'Competition is aggression!'**[7] He provides striking evidence that cooperation enhances learning much more than competition or an emphasis on individual achievement, both at school and later in life.

Hence, contrary to public opinion, research is showing us that competition is *not* the best way to go about business – thereby correcting the myth that the 'killer instinct' is necessary to succeed in the business world. This is good news, considering that 'killers' find it hard to make meaningful connections with one another! Competition puts people out of our hearts and makes them objects to conquer instead of people to love.

So what's the alternative? Futurist Riane Eisler suggests that instead of the DOMINATOR MODEL, which has prevailed in recent history, we should look at the PARTNERSHIP MODEL.[8] You may be thinking to yourself, 'Partnership is a lovely idea, but how can it work in the real world where there is so much conflict?' Yes, conflict certainly does exist; it has always existed and it always will. But conflict doesn't have to be negative; there are ways of transforming it into a source of enrichment and expansion. Up until now, our Somebody Training has taught us to handle conflict in a way that creates what looks like winners and losers. The truth is that in a competitive system there can only be losers, because in the process of trying to win we have:

1) Created a wall of separation instead of connection
2) Lost the opportunity to learn from and integrate other points of view into our own thinking
3) Adopted tunnel vision, which shuts out potentially wonderful new alternatives
4) Fed our addiction to proving we are better than someone else
5) Caused ourselves to feel more alone in the world
6) Closed our heart to the feelings of others.

I know some of you out there are still saying, 'Come now, there's nothing wrong with trying to win. Life would be so dull if there weren't the challenge of competition.' This is a common Somebody Training myth. In fact, I'd go so far as to say that most of us are addicted to competition. For example, so many of our workaholic tendencies are about being the best, winning, outdoing, proving. The fact that so many people slave away at jobs they don't like, even when they don't need the money, suggests an addiction to winning.

When we are able to let go of this addiction to competition, it is possible to jump to the level of the Higher Self and find an Everybody Training solution to conflict that is far more exciting. Here, we can begin to see conflict as opportunity for discovery. What creates conflict are the differing needs, expectations, perceptions and experiences of everyone involved. If we put all these differences in a big pot and 'play' with them long enough, we can come up with some very creative resolutions. In this way, we resolve our differences in an atmosphere of **co-creation** – people working together to come up with fresh ideas. Co-creation is much more powerful than competition. It is a win-win activity in an atmosphere of connectedness, expansion and discovery. The beauty of co-creation is that you don't have to do it alone: it's **you and me** instead of **you or me**. What a relief!

Author Merle Shain recounts this wonderful old tale which illustrates the point.[9]

'And the Lord said to the Rabbi, "Come, I will show you Hell." They entered a room where a group of people sat around a huge pot of stew. Everyone was famished and desperate. Each held a spoon that reached the pot but had a handle so long that it could not be used to reach their mouths. The suffering was terrible.

'"Come, now I will show you Heaven," the Lord said after a while. They entered another room, identical to the first – the pot of stew, the group of people, the same long spoons. But, there, everyone was happy and nourished.

'"I don't understand," said the Rabbi. "Why are they happy here when they were miserable in the other room, and everything was the same?" The Lord smiled. "Ah, but don't you see?" He said. "Here they have learned to feed each other.'"

In our effort to convert conflict into discovery, expansion and cooperation, it really helps to see ourselves as beings with very limited vision. By definition, we can see the world through our own eyes and no one else's – that's pretty limited! Conflict simply signifies that those with whom we have disagreements see with different eyes. If we get out of the way of our need to be right long enough to allow ourselves to incorporate their vision into ours, notice how much wider **our** vision becomes:

Little	**Little**	**BIGGER!**
my vision	your vision	OUR VISION!

I know this is a rather simple model, but it may help you to understand how you are limiting yourself when you have a need to be right and block out the ideas of others.

Understand that **we don't have to end up agreeing with each other**. But in the process we learn what the world looks like from different points of view. So **listen and learn** is the key to using conflict as discovery. The more we hear and the more we see, the more we allow into our internal computer and the more creative we become – and the more empathy we have for other viewpoints, thus allowing connection to occur.

We are talking about communication – and communication is essential for succeeding in the workplace (or anywhere else). Some of the ways to enhance communication in the workplace are:

1) Be open to having your belief systems changed

Each of our beliefs expresses only one point of view. Many others are just as valid. When you are constantly defending something, you can be sure a belief system is controlling the situation. Remember, a belief system is a wall that separates.

2) See other points of view as important contributions to the whole picture

Remember the old tale about the blind men describing the elephant? We are all blind men, with the option of expanding our experience and understanding if we listen carefully to others. In this way we incorporate their 'truth' into our storehouse of wisdom.

3) Agree to disagree

Not all differences require a resolution. Make your motto, 'I can live in my truth and allow you to live in your truth, respecting each of our rights to do so.' This makes it easier to arrive at solutions without anger and self-righteousness. The question then becomes, 'You have your belief and I have mine. How can we incorporate both to create a positive solution?'

4) Focus on discovery

For us perfectionists, the concept of discovery rather than achievement is a powerful one indeed. When we focus on discovery, we don't always need to be right; in fact, it sometimes serves a purpose to be wrong – we learn a new way of doing something.

5) Stop being defensive

If someone appears to 'attack' us, whatever the arena,

try to move out of the way of the attack by saying something 'disarming', such as,

- I hear what you're saying. Let's see how we can mesh our ideas.
- I'm interested in how you came to that conclusion.
- Interesting; I hadn't thought of it that way before.

. . . or something to indicate acknowledgment and an effort to understand the other person. Acknowledgment doesn't mean acquiescence. It means giving value to the other person's ideas, even if they differ from yours. Validation of this sort is a very loving act indeed.

6) Stop criticizing

When we use conflict as discovery, we no longer have to pretend we know it all. We allow others to do things their way without passing judgment, understanding that there can be many pathways to the same results.

7) Pretend you don't know anything at all

If we can let go of preconceived ideas just for a moment and pretend we're ignorant, we become much more receptive to the ideas of others.

One area in which conflict in the workplace can be seen as joyous discovery (as opposed to a battlefield) is the interaction between the sexes. At the moment, the interaction between many men and women in the workplace is still confusing, confrontive, combative and certainly competitive. This is not surprising. The roles of men and women are in the middle of a period of great change. And in a Somebody-Trained world, conflict is the natural result. Some say that change is not happening fast enough. I disagree. I feel that change is happening at an enormous rate, and if it were happening any faster the drama would be even more magnified.

Let me remind you that it was not so long ago that women were criticized for choosing to work outside the home. (I know – I was one of them!) Today, many women complain that they are criticized if they choose *not* to work outside the home. Can you understand what this tremendous shift has done to our sense of identity? Even though we are moving in the right direction, towards freedom of choice, an interim period of great confusion is inevitable.

Since conflict is the natural result of even a positive change like this, we should all consider it an opportunity for participation and growth rather than an excuse for hostility. Naturally we have to work consciously to correct any inequities and hurtful behaviour that exist. But it is important to understand that men are not the enemy of women, nor women the enemy of men. There are no enemies – there is just change. And during this time of fear and insecurity for both sexes, we need to do all that we can to keep the values of the Higher Self clearly in focus.

What is so important to understand is that *we have so much to learn from one another*. We must drop the swords, and then with awe and wonder ask each other to 'teach me about this' and 'teach me about that'. In this way we will be able to create a dynamic balance that has so far been lacking in the world of work.

The good news is that I see swords dropping and hearts opening already. It is just a matter of time before women, with dignity and self-esteem, will be 'holding up half the sky' in the workplace. It is also just a matter of time before men, with dignity and self-esteem, reduce their working hours and hold up half the sky in the raising of their children. Then children will be happier and harmony between the sexes will be restored in a world that has suffered terribly from the destructive Somebody Training practice of polarizing human roles.

Let us now commit ourselves – men and women together – to creating a 'kinder' new world of connection in the world of work.

WELCOME THE HEART INTO THE WORKPLACE

Ever since women gained the courage to march out of the house and into the workplace, there has been a natural tendency for them to buy into the DOMI-NATOR MODEL and act just like the men – believing that it was the only way to succeed. Perhaps at one time it was, but times are changing. Faster than we think, the needs of the workplace and the people in it are moving in non-traditional directions.

As discussed in the preceding section, competition, which was the mainstay of the DOMINATOR MODEL, is now being challenged by more nourishing princi-ples of connection . . . that is, traditional male values are being integrated with traditional feminine values. I believe this is a very good thing . . . *for both men and women.* The best of female values which encompass caring, compassion and working together for a common good are coming together with the best of male values which encompass strength, leadership and assertiveness. When these values meld throughout the business world, we will see the corporate bottom line moving from profit alone to a sense of personal and social responsibility.

Understand that the idea of bringing 'feminine' values into the workplace is *not* a call to arms between the sexes. In fact, many successful men have always used feminine values throughout their careers. Rather it suggests that we *all* – men and women alike – can benefit from bringing into the workplace those values of the heart that are traditionally assigned to women.

Change in this dog-eat-dog world is clearly on the horizon, and definitely in the direction of life-enhancing connection. I know change is not easy in a world where competition is almost a reflex action. We need constant reminders that there is another way. To help ease you through this transition, I've created the following EVERYBODY TRAINING ACTION VOCABULARY to take you through the work day . . . and beyond:

THE EVERYBODY TRAINING ACTION VOCABULARY

Appreciate	Validate	Empathize
Praise	Care	Share
Flow	Include	Relate
Compliment	Encourage	Reveal
Play	Relax	Balance

Explore	Commit	Cooperate
Listen	Learn	Grow
Blend	Lighten up!	Enjoy

As you can see, gone are such DOMINATOR MODEL words as compete, win, outdo, that have been so destructive to the human spirit. Keep this new action vocabulary clearly in view during the work day . . . and beyond. It will be a constant reminder of the direction in which to move your behavior. With each step that you take, simply ask yourself,

> 'Does this action embody an Everybody Training word or a Somebody Training word?'

If not, adjust your behavior accordingly. For example, if you realize that the action you are taking is one of competing, see how you can change it to one of blending.

I know that for many of you out there who are heavily involved in the proverbial 'rat race', the above sounds a bit naive. I agree that there is much yet to be done in the workplace and that sometimes our news reports make it seem as though we're moving in the wrong direction. Remember that the media tends to focus on the bad news, in business and everywhere else. As a result, we never get a chance to see all the wonderful transformations that are actually taking place. I ask, simply, that you trust that change is truly possible. More importantly, trust that YOU can be a positive force in the process. No matter what your position in the world of work, remember:

With each act of caring, you contribute to the pool of loving energy that can turn the pointless rat race into a journey of harmonious discovery.

The Soul of Connection

10

Embracing the World Like a Lover

I believe that it is our nature to connect. Starting from the deepest place within our being and expanding outwards to our family and friends, the workplace, our community and ultimately to our entire planet, I believe that we are naturally pulled forward to reach out and touch the entire world around us. I believe that, even though our training is about competing, our souls are about embracing. The only thing that stops us is the erroneous teaching of a society that has lost its way.

In the Introduction, I told you that *Dare to Connect* contains an element missing in many books of this nature. It's the very same element that's been lacking in our society – which explains very clearly why it has lost its way. As you may have already guessed, I am referring to the element of **spirituality**.

I believe that a society lacking spirituality offers no lasting solutions to the problem of alienation that envelops it. This thought can be very depressing – that is, until we ask ourselves a key question:

'Who creates society?'

The answer, of course, is:

'We do – you and I.'

This reality offers us a great deal of hope. It says that you and I can take hold of the reins and begin to steer our society out of the realm of alienation and into a place that feels more like home.

While this sounds like an impossibly difficult task, it really isn't. All that is required is that we begin our own personal journey inward to our Higher Self – the best of who we are. In so doing, we play a vital role in the transformation of society at large. As we continue to project healthier thinking and behaviour on to the planet, we, along with the countless others who have begun their own spiritual journey, can ultimately tip the scales on the side of love and light.

If you are doubtful that these countless others exist, there is considerable evidence of a dramatic shift in consciousness all around us. For example, up until recently the mention of spirituality was strongly discouraged even in self-help books such as this. It was assumed, perhaps correctly, that nobody wanted to read about it. No longer. Books with a spiritual message are hitting best-seller lists. This tells us something very encouraging:

> You and I and millions of others are finally
> paying attention to the yearning in our hearts
> for a world bathed in love rather than hate.

Little by little, the spiritual teachings of the few are reaching the hearts and minds of the many. George

Bernard Shaw once said that 'Nothing is as power[ful]
as an idea whose time has come.' I believe that the
time for a new era of spirituality, hence loving connection, has finally come – and that there is little anyone
can do to stop it, even if he or she tried!

While it is still impossible to avoid noticing the many
heartless happenings throughout the world, it is also
impossible to avoid noticing the many signs of spiritual healing. These signs are everywhere – in medi-
cine, in business, in religion, in psychology, in
education, in politics and in showbusiness. In medi-
cine we are beginning to see the melding of body, mind
and spirit in doctors' surgeries and in hospitals where
practices such as meditation and the 'laying on of
hands' are becoming more common. A new field of
psychology has been created – Transpersonal
Psychology – which uses spiritual exercises to heal
mental distress. And so on. Spirituality is in the air,
everywhere. And this fact should offer great hope to
those who desperately want to see a society guided by
the Everybody Training principles of connection and
love rather than the Somebody Training principles of
alienation, fear and competition.

Given that so little formal education as yet relates
to the spiritual, we as individuals have been given a
very unique challenge: to find our own way of creating
connection where alienation now exists. Here are a
few possibilities:

1) We can create connection where alien-ation now exists . . .

By asking the following questions of our Higher Self
as we move through each activity of our day and as
we touch the lives of those around us:

'How can I be softer and more loving?'

'How can I reach out to the people in the world around me?'

'How can I build others up and show them how wonderful they are?'

'How can I expand the bottom line of my entire life and give meaning and purpose to every action that I take?'

'How can I radiate light in a world that sometimes looks very dark?'

'How can I open my heart and take more responsibility in healing the hurts I see around me every day of my life?'

The questions are never-ending, but without them we just continue in our petty pace, healing nothing and perpetuating patterns of pain and loneliness that envelop so much of the world. It is through these poignant questions to our Higher Self that we find answers to nourish us and give us direction.

You've already discovered that in order actually to hear the wisdom of our Higher Self we need to move the Lower Self out of the way – the incessant negative chatter of our minds is not exactly conducive to great wisdom. Here is where our programme of daily spiritual exercises comes in. As I mentioned earlier, these are available to us through an enormous array of spiritual tools: affirmations, meditation, visualizations, spiritually-oriented self-help books and tapes, workshops, the principles of Aikido and so on and so on. In doing these healing exercises, we learn how to put spirit into everything we do. *The spiritual is not something out there in never-never land. It is meant to be used in our everyday lives.* The process of putting spirituality in your everyday life is really quite clear:

> *Ask your Higher Self what is the loving way of doing something, and then follow its instructions – no matter how much your Lower Self objects!*

As we keep repeating this process in more and more situations, we begin to drink in the good feelings that loving actions create. Just as importantly, we create a new kind of lifestyle (an Everybody Training kind of lifestyle) which is infused with love and caring.

Daily exercises allow us to remain conscious about the kind of energy we are sending forth into this world. Awareness is the key. Without it, we fall zombie-like into the Somebody Training habits that create separation. Awareness ultimately allows us to replace these negative actions with the positive actions of connection. And as we thus become spiritually strong, we can't help but radiate energy that is a healing force on this planet.

Our daily spiritual exercises also allow us to change our thinking. Spiritual teacher Marianne Williamson cites a wonderful line from the *Course in Miracles*:[1] 'Every thought leads you straight to Heaven or straight to Hell.'[2] It is clear that when we have Somebody Training thoughts of competing, controlling and comparing we are led straight to Hell; when we have Everybody Training thoughts about caring, sharing and loving we are led straight to Heaven. Reflect on your own thoughts, and you will see that truer words were never spoken. To change our thoughts requires, once again, to do our daily homework of replacing the 'hellish' words of our internal Chatterbox with the 'heavenly' words of the Higher Self.

Spirituality is about our Higher Self – the divine within us all. It is about expansion and growth in the direction of love, light and caring. I believe that touching the world of the spirit is our ultimate human need, the only thing that brings us a sense of wholeness and purpose in life. When we feel those exquisite moments of oneness with those around us, we can be sure we are touching that enchanted world of the spiritual. And when we are in the throes of fear and loneliness, hate and anger, you can be sure that we have lost sight of the spiritual. Therefore, the pilgrimage into the spiritual part of who we are is the most important journey we can ever take.

2) We can create connection where alienation now exists . . .

By actually visualizing ourselves projecting light into the world. Again, using the image of light is a wonderful way of radiating out our loving energy to others. Scientists have discovered that people experience much more depression in dark climates and seasons than in light ones. That makes perfect sense to me. The light of the sun has always symbolized warmth, expansiveness, touching, reaching out. So visualize light pouring forth from every pore of your body as you walk through the world each and every day of your life.

Alan Cohen tells the following story which demonstrates how simply and wondrously healing light can be used.[3] Psychologist and author Jerry Jampolsky once asked a large audience, 'Would you like to be free of your troubles?' Naturally, a big *yes* was heard throughout the room. He then invited everyone to send love and light to Joey, a little boy standing next to him who had cancer. Within moments, loving light could be felt throughout the auditorium. For that one moment in time, everyone's troubles disappeared as the light of their souls came forward to touch and warm Joey. It is said that the law of consciousness is such that our minds can hold only one thought at a time.

> When we project our light on to other beings, we *immediately* tap into the essence of connection.

3) We can create connection where alienation now exists . . .

By seeing ourselves as connected to a Higher Power – whatever that means to you. I have heard this Higher Power referred to as many things, such as God, the life force, universal law and universal light. I seriously doubt that even those of us who consider ourselves atheists have gone through life never having felt at least one sublime moment of connection with what appears to be some form of Higher Power. Perhaps we have not identified it as such, but those magical moments of oneness with something bigger than ourselves surely occur . . . for all of us.

When we find a way of connecting our energy with that of a Higher Power, the feeling of being lost in the world vanishes. Again, staying conscious to the presence of a Higher Power requires daily practice, even for devout believers.

One of my favourite meditations that gives me the sense of touching a Higher Power is quite simple and very magical in its effect.

a) I close my eyes and take in a deep breath.
b) I then imagine myself breathing out *through a*

large opening at the top of my head into a vast sky of luminous healing light.

c) Next, I imagine myself breathing in some of this luminous healing light from above *back through the opening at the top of my head* until it fills up my entire body from head to toe.

d) Finally, I imagine myself breathing out, radiating this Universal Light out into the world through my breath and through every pore in my body, touching everything as far and as wide as my mind can see.

As I repeat this process over and over again, the feeling of a wonderful cyclical connection between a Higher Power, my entire being and the rest of the world is created. This simple meditation can create a feeling of great peace and power in a very short time.

4) We can create connection where alienation now exists . . .

By caring. Caring is another way of projecting light. Acts of caring can be seen as light from the soul, and I have seen this light of the soul come forward to touch other souls in many unexpected ways.

One day as I was walking down the street in New York City I saw halfway down the block a tough-looking young man, his jacket imprinted with a skull and crossbones, swaggering arrogantly in and out of the crowd. I prejudged him as someone who wouldn't give the time of day to anyone on the street – not that anyone would dare to ask! At one point, his eye caught sight of a blind old man with a cane, tottering precariously towards the kerb. Without thinking, he ran forward and headed the old man off before any damage was done. Then he took off once again. After he had progressed a little way, he turned back to see if the old man was keeping on a straight course. No, he was once again headed for the kerb. The young man darted back and impatiently told the old man he was still going toward the kerb. But to no avail. Yet again, the old man went off course. Finally, with a nod of resignation, our tough guy teamed up with the little old man, and this very unlikely couple proceeded nobly down the street . . . together. Magical! A moment of connection. A moment of the divine. (And an eye-opener to me about judging people by their appearance!)

How easy it is to bring the light of the Spirit forth!

> One simple act of caring and the whole world
> is transformed right before our very eyes.

Everyone is touched, uplifted and comforted. Everyone connects with love. So why are acts of caring not glaringly abundant in our society? There are a few possible answers to this elusive question.

a) **To care** requires us to keep our heart open. When our heart is open, we 'feel' the blind man's darkness, the starving child's hunger, the sick woman's suffering. For many of us, these feelings are far too painful; we would rather shut them out and not care so much.

But when all is said and done, it is our openness to other people's feelings that allows us to touch the soul within. It allows us to touch our own pain. It allows compassion. It allows a world in which there are truly no strangers.

And, ultimately, we learn that the pain does not wipe us out. It strengthens us. It allows us to walk positively forward, knowing that we can learn from all of life's experiences . . . and so can everyone else, despite what hardships befall them.

b) **To care** requires responsibility. Many of us don't want this responsibility. We're too preoccupied with Somebody Training ideas of success. We're busy earning a living, rushing through life, wondering when it will all begin to feel good. We don't have time to care. In that, we miss the boat. Thankfully, more boats keep coming back to offer us another opportunity to join the human family . . . and ultimately to understand what feeling good *really* means.

c) **To care** involves the possibility that someone needs help from us, and many of us don't want to be needed. We don't want to grow up. We haven't yet discovered that it is soul-destroying to remain forever a child. It is only when we finally make the jump into adulthood that we discover the unmatched joy of contributing to someone else's life in our own unique way.

One dilemma we all face when we finally do grow up is that there is so much 'caring' to be done in the world. How do we cope with it all? We begin by understanding that *we don't have to do it all.* We take it one step at a time, acting only on those situations that intuitively pull us in their direction and letting the rest go, trusting that others will be there to say yes where we have said no.

d) **To care** requires making the gift of ourselves, and some of us feel we have nothing to offer. How much opportunity for connecting we miss by thinking such a powerless thought! We all have something to offer, whatever our circumstances.

I knew of a woman in New York who was confined to her bed. What did she have to offer? She asked her Higher Self the same question and came up with a wonderful answer. She had a telephone and she still had a voice. Through a social services agency she obtained a list of other bedridden people, and spent most of her waking hours calling these people just to let them know that somebody cared. Many of them became her 'phone friends'.

It takes so little – just a little attention off the self, the opportunity to say to someone else, 'Hello, I'm here. How can I help you on your journey on this very strange planet?'

> To care is automatically to become at one with another soul.

We can bring a quality of caring to all our human exchanges, whatever they may be. We innately thirst for the feelings that come from acts of caring. They make us feel useful, connected, spiritually whole. Acts of caring make life worth living. A life of emptiness could be transformed by a life of caring.

5) We can create connection where alienation now exists . . .

By creating a feeling of family with the world of 'strangers' around us. With today's Somebody Training focus on materialism, success and getting ahead, we have lost the sense of comfort that a sense of family can bring.

One way of enhancing the feeling of family around

us is to stop, wherever we can, the *us versus them* mentality that pervades our Somebody-Trained society. We need to stay conscious when politicians talk about *them*, when the media talk about *them*, when our friends and family talk about *them*. We need to stay conscious when we hear statements such as 'Why should we feed people over there when there are people starving over here?'

> In a world where there are no strangers, there is no 'over there'. There is only all of us . . . everywhere . . . one human family!

One of the most poignant expressions of this philosophy was that made by the Labour politician Tony Benn, who, as young men were being brought home from the Falklands War in coffins draped with the Union Jack, said, 'We can't kill over flags any more.' No, we can't, not if we hope to achieve spiritual wholeness and survive as a planet. Nothing is so damaging to our inner sense of connection than an us-versusthem kind of message. We need to be constantly on watch so that a new kind of thinking can be brought forth on to this planet – the kind of thinking that creates only connection and love. And as we begin to look deep inside, we notice that all our longing pulls us in that direction.

6) We can create connection where alienation now exists . . .

By committing ourselves to something about which we feel very deeply – the environment, literacy, hunger, peace, a community project, whatever – knowing that we are important members of this global family. If you don't believe that you are important, act as if you were. Ask yourself,

> *'If I were really an important member of this global family, what would I be doing?'*

And then proceed to do it one step at a time. You will be amazed at how much distance your loving light can cover in this step-by-step process.

7) We can create connection where alienation now exists . . .

By making our spiritual growth a lifelong commitment. Yes, it does take that long – perhaps longer! I know of no one who has yet achieved enlightenment 100 per cent. Even our great spiritual teachers continually laugh at their own lapses into the realm of the ego or Lower Self. They, too, have the need to monitor their thoughts, words and behaviour *daily*. Once again we see that 'there are no strangers' even among our greatest teachers.

Learning the art of patience is part of our spiritual journey. The world does not change overnight, nor do we. For all of us, it is a constant process of learning and growing. It is a process of using all life's experiences to show us the way home. **And with each step forward, we come closer to the truth of our own magnificence**.

The road to connection is clear. It begins inside and radiates out to everyone around us in an ever-growing beam of light. Perhaps it will help make those first few steps of the journey easier when we understand that creating a feeling of connection, first with ourselves and then with others, is the most important thing we can do.

Rabbi Kushner was watching two children building sandcastles at the water's edge. Just when they had finished an elaborate castle that had taken much time and patience to build, a wave came along and knocked it down. He expected tears and upset. Instead they sat there laughing and holding hands and soon began building another castle. He said . . .

> 'I realized they had taught me an important lesson. All the things in our lives, all the complicated structures we spend so much time and energy creating are built on sand. Only our relationships to other people endure. Sooner or later, the wave will come along and knock down what we have worked so hard to build up. When that happens, only the person who has somebody's hand to hold will be able to laugh.'[4]

Think carefully about this last quote. It says something very significant about building a life filled with love.

And so we come to the end of *Dare to Connect*. And to you who are reading this book at this very moment, I say the same thing that was said to me many years ago: 'I don't know your name; but I know who you are.' And,

> Who you are is someone who has the power within to create a Heaven on earth for yourself and to radiate a piece of that Heaven out to everyone whose life touches yours.

There will be times when you forget this important truth. So to help you imprint it permanently in your mind, I'd like you to write the following sentence on a little card, carry it with you wherever you go, and read it at least ten times every single day of your life from this day forth:

> *'Who I am is someone who has the power within to create a Heaven on earth for myself and to radiate a piece of that Heaven out to everyone whose life touches mine.'*

Say it out loud now. Say it again. Say it yet again. Feel the bliss inherent in such an awesomely powerful message. Repeat it over and over again for as many days, months or years as it takes until you fully feel it, hear it, breathe it, see it, walk it and talk it – that is, until you finally take in its implications and begin consciously to live your life within its truth. In that, you will find an unending surge of joy, light and love that will nourish and support you all the days of your life.

Appendix:

A guided visualization for connecting with confidence

A guided visualization is a powerful way to tap into parts of your being that are usually clouded by the negative mind. It is designed to help you get in touch with your Higher Self – the part of you that is loving, creative, intuitive, joyful, giving, abundant, the part of you that knows *there is nothing to fear*.

A guided visualization is most effective in an audio format; therefore, I suggest you softly, gently, and *very* slowly speak the following into a tape recorder. If you find your own voice too distracting, ask a friend to speak it into a tape recorder for you. I've provided dotted lines to indicate where there should be silence on the tape to allow time for the instructions to be followed. (A good tip is to speak more slowly and leave more time for the instructions than you think are necessary.)*

* I've recorded a similar guided visualisation at the end of my CD entitled *The Art of Fearbusting*. You can order this CD at www.susanjeffers.com.

You need to set the stage. Select a time when you are unlikely to be disturbed. You may even want to take the telephone off the hook. Find yourself a comfortable position, either lying down, or sitting in a chair with a straight spine, both feet on the floor and hands in your lap.

As you listen to the instructions, *don't try to monitor the thoughts or pictures that come into your head,* even if they seem silly. Some of you may not see anything at all. Not to worry. Visualizations are very effective for some, but not for everyone. Relax, knowing there are many other ways to access the Higher Self such as with the use of affirmations or meditation. Also don't be upset if you get a negative picture. Sometimes negative pictures tell us as much as the positive ones. Just look for the message that is being given you and make it a learning experience. You may find yourself dozing off. That's OK, too. Just try again another day.

The following is a guided visualization designed to allow you greater ease in connecting with yourself and everyone around you. It is meant to enhance your feeling of power and love and to help you step comfortably into any type of social situation. Here are the words for your audio recorder:

Find yourself a comfortable position and close your eyes . . .

Take a very deep breath . . . and then let go . . .

Once again, take another deep breath and feel the energy coursing throughout your body . . . and let go . . .

Take another deep breath, this time imagining yourself breathing in the loving light of the Universe . . . and as you release, see yourself breathing out loving light into the Universe . . .

Enjoy the peace of just being there . . . having nothing to do but to listen to these words. Ignore the sounds around you as well as the unrelated thoughts that come into your head . . . Allow what comes up for you to come up.

Begin to relax your body . . . from the top of your head to the tips of your toes . . . relax . . . between your eyes . . . relax . . . Relax your cheeks . . . your jaw . . . your neck . . . your shoulders . . . arms . . . relax . . .

Take another deep breath and feel yourself relaxing all over . . . your chest . . . your back . . . stomach . . . thighs . . . calves . . . ankles . . . feet . . . Let it all go . . .

Take one more deep breath and if you are still holding tension in any area of your body, just let go . . .

Now . . . in your mind's eye, imagine yourself getting ready to go to some social event . . . It could be a party, a meeting, a class or whatever your mind envisions . . .

See yourself dressing up for the occasion . . . and as you look into the mirror, see a loving and confident you, the **you** you always wanted to be. Smile as you get a sense, not of your physical beauty, but the richness and warmth that you hold inside . . .

As you look into the mirror, you are instilled with a wonderful sense of confidence. You feel your own power, your own ability to love, and you know that you have something to offer everyone you meet . . . Really get into those feelings of power, confidence and love . . .

And as you stand in front of that mirror, affirm to yourself:

I am a powerful and loving person and I have much to give. I am creating light wherever I go.

Really experience the power in those words . . .

Stand tall . . . and look into your eyes seeing only the beauty that lies within . . . the part of you that is loving, giving and caring. Breathe in those feelings, knowing this part of you really exists . . .

Take a moment to enjoy that beautiful image in the mirror . . .

Now transport yourself to the door of this special event and look inside . . . See all the assembled guests . . . and, as you stand there, once again allow yourself to feel your own magnificence . . .

This time affirm to yourself:

I am a beautiful person. My purpose here today is to make others feel good about who they are.

Allow yourself to feel confident, self-assured, caring and loving, knowing that you have your own special contribution to bring to the people in the room . . .

Let yourself experience the power and love that come from that knowledge . . .

Standing tall and confident, step inside knowing that you are a very valuable member of this group . . . and begin interacting with the people in the room . . .

Feel what it would feel like to have no fear of rejection, no self-consciousness, only focusing outward to the people in the room . . .

With this sense of confidence, what would you be doing? . . . See yourself making others feel at ease, knowing they are probably nervous and insecure . . . See yourself interested, caring, and sensitive to their insecurity . . . What would you be doing? Really look at yourself . . .

Look at the love in your own heart . . . Realize that everybody in the room wants to connect. They want to feel loved and accepted . . . just like you. Remember, there truly are no strangers . . .

Just knowing you have so much to give takes away the fear . . . You feel comfortable . . . flowing . . . See yourself   interacting . . . giving . . . asking . . . loving . . . listening . . . caring . . .

Now look around . . . How would others be reacting to you when you are confident and loving? . . . What would they be doing? . . . See them interacting with you . . . What does it look like? . . . What would you be doing now, caring about others, being interested in others? . . . Watch yourself . . . and watch how others are reacting to you.

See yourself the way you'd like to be . . . and know that you can create this picture in reality . . . Slowly but strongly, you can build your confidence . . . You can train your mind to see your true nature . . . the loving person that you are . . .

Enjoy being in this room for a few more seconds . . . Look at the love around you . . . Look at the love in your own heart . . . Realize that everyone in the room wants to connect . . . They want to feel whole . . . They want to feel love just as you do . . . and you have the capacity to contribute to their lives . . .

Bathe in the feeling of belonging for just a few moments . . .

And when you are ready, start to bring yourself back into the room . . . Be aware of your body . . .

Start to move around and stretch . . .

Take a deep breath knowing that you can return to this place any time you wish . . . And when you are ready, open your eyes.

And as you 'come back' from this healing and peaceful way of being, it might be helpful to write down any observations you might have had which may be of future value to you. If you feel you learned from this visualization, repeat it frequently. Do it before any social gathering. It will bolster your self-confidence enormously and remind you of how much love you have to give to this world.

Chapter Notes

Note: Some of these resources may no longer be available. Not to worry! There are so many wonderful resources available today to help you on your journey to self-discovery. And it is a wonderful journey indeed!

Chapter 1
1. Ram Dass, *Who Are You*, The Soundworks, Inc. (Audiotape)
2. Bradshaw, John, *Healing the Shame that Binds You*, Health Communications, Inc., 1988, p. vii.
3. Powell, John, *Why Am I Afraid To Tell You Who I Am?*, Zondervan Publishing House, New Edition, 1999, p. 134.

Chapter 2
1. *Losing a Love . . . Finding a Life* is now available as an e-book. Go to www.susanjeffers.com. It truly is a diary of my journey from a sense of emptiness to a sense of wholeness after the breakup of my first marriage many, many years ago.

Chapter 3

1. Cohen, Alan, *Rising in Love: The Journey Into Light*, Eden Company in cooperation with Coleman Graphics, 1983, p. 143.

2. Powell, John, *Why Am I Afraid to Tell You Who I Am?*, Zondervan Publishing House, New Edition, 1999, p. 12.

3. Many additional self-esteem exercises can be found in most of my other books including *The Feel the Fear Guide to Lasting Love* (Vermilion, 2007), *Feel the Fear and Do it Anyway*® 20th Year Edition (Vermilion, 2007), *Feel the Fear . . . and Beyond*, (Vermilion, 2000), *Opening Our Hearts to Men* (Piatkus Books, 2005), *Embracing Uncertainty* (Hodder Mobius, 2003), and *End the Struggle and Dance with Life*, (Hodder Mobius, 2005).

4. Weltner, Linda, 'The Miracle of Imperfection', *New Age Journal*, September/October, 1990, p. 136.

5. The three calming affirmation CDs I have created to get rid of negativity and to build self-confidence are *Inner Talk for Peace of Mind, Inner Talk for a Confident Day*, and *Inner Talk for a Love that Works*. To order these CDs go to www.susanjeffers.com.

6. Broadbent, W. W., *How to Be Loved*, Prentice-Hall, New York, 1976, pp. 28–43.

7. Bradshaw, John, *Healing the Shame that Binds You*, Health Communications, Inc., 1988, p. 14.

8. You can find more information about Co-Dependents Anonymous-UK (CoDA UK) at www.coda-uk.org which explains that 'CoDA is a set of informal self-help groups made up of men and women with a common interest in working through the problems that co-dependency has caused in their lives.'

9. Two books that describe the process of inner-child work are *Healing Your Aloneness: Finding Love And Wholeness Through Your Inner Child* by Erika Chopich and Margaret Paul (Harper and Row, San Francisco, 1990) and *Home Coming: Reclaiming And Championing Your Inner Child* by John Bradshaw (Piatkus Books, 1990).

Chapter 4

1. Tanner, Ira, *Loneliness: The Fear Of Love*, Perennial Library, Harper and Row, New York, 1973, p. 48.
2. Lindbergh, Anne Morrow, *Gift From The Sea*, Chatto and Windus, New Edition, 1992, p. 42.
3. Nouwen, Henri J.M., *Out Of Solitude*, Ave Marie Press, Revised Edition 2004, p. 22.
4. To learn more about The Inside Edge, go to www.insideedge.org.
5. As I mentioned in Chapter 2, *Losing a Love . . . Finding a Life*, which is a 'diary' of my journey from lost to found, is available as an e-book at www.susanjeffers.com.

Chapter 5

1. 'Imaginary' healing light can be used in many ways: to soothe diseased parts of the body, make you feel more peaceful, create more harmony in your life, and help you reach out to others. You might want to investigate further. Sanaya Roman includes a chapter entitled 'Creating With Light' in her book *Spiritual Growth*, H.J. Kramer, Inc., 1989.
2. Wilde, Stuart, *Affirmations*, Hay House, 1987, p. 37.
3. Carnegie, Dale, *How To Win Friends And Influence People*, Vermilion, New Edition, 2007, p. 66.

4. Canfield, Jack, *Self-Esteem: Your Key To Success.* (Audio-tape)

5. Trine, Ralph Waldo, *In Tune With The Infinite,* Wilder Publications Limited, 2007, p. 2. (Originally published in 1899 by G. Bell and Son Ltd.)

Chapter 6

1. Saint-Exupery, Antoine de, *The Little Prince,* Egmont, New Edition, 1991, p. 70.

2. Jeffers, Susan, *Feel The Fear And Do It Anyway®,* Vermilion, 20th Anniversary Edition, 2007, p. 135–149.

3. In *The Feel the Fear Guide to Lasting Love,* (Vermilion, 2007), I explain the important difference between 'instant love' and 'real love'.

4. Burns, David, *Intimate Connections,* A Signet Book, New American Library, New York, 1985, p.xvi.

5. Jeffers, Susan, *Opening Our Hearts To Men,* Piatkus, New Edition, 2005. p. 57.

Chapter 7

1. Keen, Sam, *The Passionate Life: Stages Of Loving,* HarperCollins, Australia, 1984, pp. 216–217.

2. Prosapio, Richard (Coyote), in 'The Men's Movement' by Valentine Riddell, *Santa Fe Spirit Magazine,* August/September, 1990, p. 22.

3. Friends in Recovery, *The 12 Steps: A Way Out: A Spiritual Process for Healing Damaged Emotions,* Recovery Publications, Inc., Revised Edition, 1995.

Chapter 8

1. Druck, Ken (with James C. Simmons), *The Secrets*

Men Keep: Breaking The Silence Barrier, Ballantine Books, Reprint Edition, 1990, p. 144.

2. Keen, Sam, *The Passionate Life: Stages Of Loving*, HarperCollins, 1983, p. 121.

3. Found in: McGill, Michael E., *The McGill Report On Male Intimacy*, HarperCollins, Reprint Edition, 1986, p. 173.

4. In *Opening Our Hearts To Men* (Piatkus, 2005), I discuss our lagging expectations and ways we can catch up more quickly. (pp. 71–96) (Men, this is for you as well.)

5. Found in: Blooston, George, 'Is There a Wild Man in Your Life?', in *New Woman*, July, 1990, p. 77.

6. Ibid., p. 74.

7. Cohen, Alan, *Rising In Love: The Journey Into Light*, Eden Company in cooperation with Coleman Graphics, 1983, p. 126.

Chapter 9

1. Ram Dass, *Beyond Success*, from a workshop entitled 'On Work, Money And Burnout', Hanuman Tape Library, 1989. (Audiotape)

2. Found in: 'Seeking the Soul of Capitalism' by Charles Simpkinson, *Common Boundary Magazine*, July/August, 1990, P. 31.

3. Donald Marrs, *Executive in Passage*, Barrington Sky Publishing, 1990, p. 244.

4. To learn more about Aikido, read *The Magic Of Conflict* by Thomas F. Crum (Pocket Books, 2nd Revised Edition, 1999).

5. Jeffers, Susan, *Feel The Fear And Do It Anyway®*, Vermilion, 20th Anniversary Edition, 2007, pp. 181–201.

6. Kohn, Alfie, *No Contest: The Case Against Competition*, Houghton Mifflin Co., Boston, 2nd Revised Edition, 1993.
7. Kohn, Alfie, 'The Case Against Competition', *Noetic Sciences Review*, Spring, 1990, p. 18.
8. Eisler, Riane, *The Chalice And The Blade*, HarperCollins, Australia, 1998, p. xvii.
9. Shain, Merle, *Hearts That We Broke Long Ago*, Bantam Books, New York, 1985, p. 71.

Chapter 10

1. *A Course In Miracles* is a self-study program of spiritual healing. It is published by the Foundation for Inner Peace, P.O. Box 598, Mill Valley, CA 94942. Marianne Williamson is one of its spokespersons.
2. Williamson, Marianne, *Cosmic Adulthood*, Miracle Projects. (Audiotape)
3. Cohen, Alan, *Rising in Love: The Journey Into Light*, Eden Company in cooperation with Coleman Graphics, 1983, pp. 133–134.
4. Kushner, Harold, *When All You've Ever Wanted Isn't Enough*, Fireside, New Edition, 2002, pp. 165–166.

About the Author

Susan Jeffers, Ph.D., dubbed 'the Queen of Self-Help' by *The Times*, is considered one of the top self-help authors in the world. Her books have been published in over 100 countries and translated into over 36 languages. *Feel the Fear and Do It Anyway*® launched her career as a best-selling author. Some of her many other titles include *Feel the Fear and Beyond, End the Struggle and Dance With Life, Embracing Uncertainty, Opening our Hearts to Men, The Feel the Fear Guide to Lasting Love, and Life is Huge!*. She is a much sought after media personality. She lives with her husband in Los Angeles, California.

For more information, visit www.susanjeffers.com.

Also by Susan Jeffers:

OPENING OUR HEARTS TO MEN

Taking charge of our lives and creating a love that works

Susan Jeffers

Susan Jeffers has helped millions of people throughout the world overcome their fears, heal their relationships, and move forward in life with confidence and love. In *Opening Our Hearts to Men* she shares her own experiences, and offers wisdom, insights and practical advice on how to feel good about yourself and your relationships.

Opening Our Hearts to Men is a book for every woman who wants to bring more love into her life. It will help you if:

- Your relationship is not working out in the way you had hoped
- You want to develop greater intimacy in your relationships
- You find it difficult to form lasting relationships with men
- You are feeling lonely and unloved

'Finally a book that doesn't make men the enemy, but offers women practical tips for creating the loving relationships we deserve' Barbara de Angeles, author of *How To Make Love All The Time*

'A brilliant book and I wish I had published it myself . . .' Louise L. Hay, author of *You Can Heal Your Life*

978-0-7499-2644-1

Also from Piatkus:

THE HOW OF HAPPINESS

A practical guide to getting the life you want

Sonja Lyubomirsky

We all want to be happier – it's what makes life worth living – but few of us know how to go about improving our happiness.

Revealing that a startling 40 per cent of our capacity for happiness is within our power to change, Sonja Lyubomirsky guides us through the many obstacles to happiness as well as the methods to harness out individual strengths to overcome them.

Charting new territory in the science of happiness and using groundbreaking diagnostic tests, Sonja Lyubomirsky tailors the wealth of her research to you individual personality, resources, goals and needs. *The How of Happiness* demystifies the many myths that complicate the pursuit of happiness and provides the straightforward steps to finding sustained happiness and a more fulfilling, productive and enjoyable life.

978-0-7499-5246-4